Paths to Peace

The Henry Rolfs Book Series
of the
Institute of Noetic Sciences

Higher Creativity:
Liberating the Unconscious Mind
for Breakthrough Insights
Willis Harman and
Howard Rheingold

Waking Up:
Overcoming the Obstacles
to Human Potential
Charles T. Tart

The Noetic Sciences Book Series is dedicated to Henry Rolfs, a long-standing member of the Board of Directors, whose leadership, generosity, and personal courage have been instrumental in establishing the Institute of Noetic Sciences.

About the Book and Authors

A primer on thinking about peace in a nuclear age, this book describes the kinds of peace efforts that have been tried—and those that might be tried—from the highest echelons of government policymaking to the grassroots level of individual endeavor. Its primary goal is to enable the reader to understand ways of eliminating the threat of nuclear war and to be empowered to take action.

The book describes and compares nine basic methods people have used to achieve peace, ranging from such conventional approaches as the theories of deterrence and balance of power to more unconventional strategies such as nonviolent resistance. Essentially all significant ideas for achieving and maintaining international peace fall into one of these nine categories or combine features from several. Many have been tried, but all clearly have been found wanting.

Yet the authors' tone is one of optimism as they explore some of the major changes of the past quarter century. They contend that these changes alter the balance of advantages and disadvantages among the various paths to peace, so that what seemed partially workable in the past may not be appropriate to the present and what seemed totally impractical in the past might have a chance of working today. The book concludes with a scenario that may make a stable peace possible in the foreseeable future.

Richard Smoke is professor of political science and research director, Center for Foreign Policy Development, Brown University. **Willis Harman** is president of the Institute of Noetic Sciences, Sausalito, California.

Published in cooperation with
the Institute of Noetic Sciences

Paths to Peace

Exploring the Feasibility of Sustainable Peace

Richard Smoke
with Willis Harman

Westview Press / Boulder and London

Copyright © 1987 by the Institute of Noetic Sciences

Published in 1987 in the United States of America by Westview Press, Inc.; Frederick A. Praeger, Publisher; 5500 Central Avenue, Boulder, Colorado 80301

Library of Congress Cataloging-in-Publication Data
Smoke, Richard.
  Paths to peace.
  Includes index.
  1. Peace. 2. Nuclear arms control. I. Harman,
Willis W. II. Title.
JX1952.S686 1987   327.1′72   87-2173
ISBN 0-8133-0492-X
ISBN 0-8133-0487-3 (pbk.)

Composition for this book was provided by the authors.

Printed and bound in the United States of America

6   5   4   3   2   1

Contents

Preface   ix
Acknowledgments   xiv

Introduction   1

    What Is Peace?   1
    Nine Paths to Peace   3
    About This Book   5

1   Traditional Paths to Coping with Conflict   7

    The Path of Removing the Threat   7
    The Path of Deterrence   10
    Summary   16

2   Traditional Paths to Preventing Conflict   17

    The Path of Preventive Diplomacy   18
    The Path of Disarmament and Arms Control   24
    The Path of Removing Fundamental Causes of War   31
    Summary   37

3   Alternative Paths to Coping with Conflict   39

    The Path of Alternative Defense   40
    The Path of Nonviolent Action   47

4   Alternative Paths to Preventing Conflict   55

    The Path of Alternative Conflict Resolution   55
    The Path of Changing Attitudes:
       The Delegitimation of War   62

The Combination of Changing Attitudes and
   Alternative Conflict Resolution   65
Recapitulation   67

5   The Possibility of Peace   73

Degrees of Peace   73
The Belief in Possibility   75
Toward the Belief in Possibility   76
Some Elements of an Image   78
The Importance of Attitudes   80
The Realism of Believing in Peace   81
The Power of Understanding the Psyche   82
The Plausibility of Transformative Change   87
The Shape of the Next Age   90
Reassessing the Possibility of Peace   95
Conclusion   97

Notes   101
For Further Reading   103
Index   107

Preface

by Willis Harman

The existence of nuclear weapons has presented us with a requirement for 100 percent reliability that is found nowhere else in human affairs. Human civilization cannot survive even one global nuclear war. In this sense our endeavor to achieve lasting peace and common security must succeed.

One might think that with this unprecedented challenge before us, there would be no effort spared in pursuit of the goal; that both governments and individual citizens would be unrelenting and single-minded in our common hour of need. Yet such is not the case. Our "national security" policies are confused and most certainly do not provide a feeling of security. Our stance toward peace is ambivalent and indecisive; in some circles the word "peace" has taken on connotations of weakness or of empathy with the Soviets. Much of the public seems disinterested, apathetic, and resigned or feels powerless to take effective action. Few people feel capable of thinking clearly about the issue; few have confidence in the ability of their leaders to guide them wisely toward a peaceful future.

It is this situation that is addressed by this book. We who are alive today, and whose future world is so at risk, typically do not think clearly about peace. Even the definition of the word is not thought through when we speak or write about peace. That is why this book is written as a primer. It is sophisticated, but simple.

The conviction that permeates the book is that peace and the general security of all are attainable goals. But to achieve them will require *a whole-system change:* the combined efforts of vast numbers of people around the globe thinking clearly about the issues and committing themselves to achieving those critically important goals. Paradoxically, the need for a whole-system change does not necessarily make the goal appear less achievable—whole-system change has happened before and could happen again—but rather indicates the kinds of actions that are likely to be effective.

A brief summary will adequately serve to remind us of what is almost obvious: Peace is a whole-system issue. The production of weaponry was once carried on almost exclusively by governments for their own use; commerce in weapons between nations was considered highly unethical. The manufacture and sale of weapons now represents a significant segment of the U.S. economy, and the economic repercussions of a serious cutback in military production could be severe, at least temporarily. The continuing military buildup has a momentum all its own. Part of that momentum is the psychological inertia of conventional ways of thinking about international conflict.

In the United States, the immediate point of conflict appears to center around the fear of communism and involves not just the NATO countries versus the Warsaw Pact countries; the rest of the world is part of the conflict as well. And the fear is not only that territory may be taken by force but also that noncapitalist ideas may gain hold in other parts of the world. (The wisest response to that threat would seem to be to make sure that the free enterprise system works so well for everybody that alternative systems have no appeal. Unfortunately, when we are fearful we do not always take the wisest course.)

There is an implicit assumption in most discussions of peace that the Soviet Union is the "enemy" of permanent concern. But North-South tensions are likely to long outlast that particular temporary conflict. The rich capitalist countries require ever-increasing consumption for the well-being of their economies, yet the planet would be hard-pressed to accommodate all five or six billion people in mass-consumption societies. On the other hand, it is hard to imagine a state of peace on the planet when the vast majority of people remain in a condition of relative privation while the minority strives to increase consumption to maintain flourishing economies. This issue of the relationship between the consuming minority in the rich nations and the far-poorer vast majority of the Earth's population is likely to remain long after the Soviet Union and the United States have learned to coexist.

These connections among the various pieces of the world's complex macroproblem become fairly obvious when we turn our attention to them. But we often overlook how completely our predicament is a direct consequence of a way of thinking that emerged in Western Europe only a few centuries ago. To quote Roger Walsh:

Moreover, for the first time in millions of years of human evolution, all the major threats to our survival are human-caused. Problems such as nuclear weapons, pollution, and ecological imbalance stem directly from our own behavior and can therefore be traced to psychological origins. This means that the current threats to human survival and well-being are *actually symptoms,* symptoms of our individual and shared mind-set.[1]

The problems, in other words, are not only connected, but have a common source in the underlying Western perspectives and tacit assumptions that have shaped not only science and technology, but practically all aspects of modern society.

An analogy will help make the point. It is well known that many illnesses are related to an underlying condition of stress, which has among its effects the impairment of the body's immune system. When these diseases (such as peptic ulcers, allergies, and cardiovascular disease) are considered as isolated problems, the attempts to heal often fail—or result in another symptom popping up somewhere else. The reason is that the underlying cause has not been dealt with. It might seem that dealing with the whole collection of possible illnesses and their underlying cause all at once would necessarily be far more complex than approaching one of them alone. But this is not so. Changing the attitudinal approach to life and eliminating stress is in principle quite simple. (It may *appear* hard because of the psychological resistance to deep inner change.) Treating the whole-system problem of stress is more successful than direct attacks on the separate medical problems.

The analogy suggests that the nuclear weapons threat, global environmental problems, world poverty and hunger, and an assortment of other modern dilemmas relate to an underlying mind-set in such a way that none of them are solvable without a change in that mind-set. Yet with that change and the associated whole-system change they all become solvable.

The analogy fits in one more way as well. Just as the executive with heart trouble may be more accepting of a diagnosis that leads to bypass surgery than of one that requires a change in his or her fundamental attitudes, so many people today will seek for a resolution of the peace issue *almost anywhere* except in a fundamental change of mind.

But is whole-system change a plausible scenario? There are two points to be made. First, there is precedent: Whole-system change has happened before in history. Second, forces that might bring this change about are increasingly in evidence.

Within the context of Western civilization alone there have been at least two whole-system changes: the end of the Greco-Roman world and the transition from the Middle Ages, through the Renaissance and Reformation periods, into the modern age. It might seem rash indeed to predict a similarly profound revolutionary transfiguration of society. Yet a substantial and growing number of writers and thinkers do predict it, and there are some signs that make such a scenario not so unreasonable an expectation. Having lived over forty years with nuclear weapons, we are increasingly aware of the awfulness of our situation. Slowly but surely people are building up opposition to continuing the same perilous trends.

The facts of those trends are familiar but still staggering. The total number of nuclear weapons in the world is around 50,000, with a total explosive power about two million times that of the Hiroshima bomb and a total tonnage 7,000 times that of all the bombs dropped during World War II. The explosion of even one of these weapons would be likely to release radioactive fallout that would dwarf the impact of Chernobyl to insignificance. Global nuclear war would result in devastation and suffering on a scale totally unknown in human history. The biological consequences, immediate and long-range, have been estimated and would be severe.

Even if nuclear weapons were never again to be exploded, the radioactive waste already generated by their manufacture remains as an unsolved problem. Thousands of tons of radioactive waste products contain substances that are likely to remain toxic for centuries; no way is known to render the waste harmless, and no leak-proof storage has been devised.

Economically, the arms race is a drain on all nations, most especially on the two superpowers and many of the Third World countries. Global military expenditures currently run around a trillion dollars a year, which is nearly three billion dollars a day. A small fraction of this expenditure could provide the whole world with adequate nutrition and sanitary water supply, public health measures to reduce disease, and housing and education.

Worldwide, military expenditures account for around 6 percent of the gross economic product. For the United States the figure is about 7 percent, for the Soviet Union around 14 percent, and for some of the Third World countries it is well above 20 percent. In some Third World countries more is being spent on armaments than on health care, education, and welfare all together. In addition to the tragic waste of resources and human effort, uncountable human deaths are resulting from malnutrition and disease, partly from the lack of preventive measures. Untold human misery in poverty-stricken countries directly results from the diversion of attention to arms.

Faced with such evidence of the effects of military buildup, people are beginning to see the need for change. Chapter 5 discusses further reasons why it may not be implausible to suppose that another fundamental change is now in the offing.

As awareness of the frightening dimensions of the nuclear dilemma has grown, people have banded together in a variety of peace organizations—and hoped that their efforts toward a nuclear freeze, or a peace academy, or a test ban treaty, might be successful. In recent years leaders in these peace-related movements have found common cause with leaders of other groups—ecological and environmental movements, "Green politics," women's movements, human rights organizations, and so on. And all of them have become more sophisticated in their understanding of how deep are the roots of the problems they are attempting to ameliorate.

At the same time a new vision has been forming: a vision of a world with nuclear disarmament and global security, appreciation of the diversity of Earth's many cultures, wholesome relationships between humans and the planet, elimination of subtle and not-so-subtle oppression of minorities and women, fundamental rights that are guaranteed by universal agreement—a vision of a world at peace. If the forces with this vision continue to grow, they could bring about the sort of whole-system change spoken of earlier. This possibility is not without hazards. People can be very fearful of change, and their reactionary responses can also bring on social disruption and human misery.

Thus there are two compelling reasons for thinking about peace in a lucid and fundamental way: (1) to be more effective in working toward peace; (2) to better understand the kind of societal trauma that we may experience during the transition period that probably lies ahead. This short book aspires to be of assistance in that task of learning to think about peace rationally, penetratingly, but still with passion.

In past conflicts we have been able to convince ourselves that if we could once vanquish the German "Huns"—or the Axis Powers, or "Red China," or the Soviets—then peace would be assured. But this logic is not as satisfying now as it was in our more naive years. We suspect that the solution to the problem is more complex than subduing some particular "enemy." The solution also involves more than choosing the right arms control policies or the right alternative security strategies or than adopting the latest conflict resolution techniques.

Yet peace and common security, for all the world and for generations to come, is a conceivable goal—and therefore an achievable goal. To achieve it we will need a lot of clear thinking about the problem; we hope this book will contribute to that. And as the book points out, the first step in achieving this goal, as with any other goal, is to *believe it can be done.*

Acknowledgments

The basic concept for a book of this kind came from the Institute of Noetic Sciences, which supported its writing with a grant to Peace and Common Security (PACS), an institute for research and education headquartered in San Francisco. Richard Smoke was executive director of PACS during the initial writing period; much of the planning and conceptualization of the book, and the bulk of the writing, were his. Midway through the project he accepted the position of research director of the Center for Foreign Policy Development at Brown University, and the work was completed there. Willis Harman, as president of the Institute of Noetic Sciences, collaborated in the conceptualization and contributed minor portions of the writing. We acknowledge with thanks the secretarial and other support of all three organizations.

Special thanks are given to Henry and Zoe Rolfs, members of the Board of the Institute of Noetic Sciences, for their financial support and encouragement. Helpful suggestions and critique of the final manuscript were provided by Mark Garrison and Dietrich Fischer. Sharon Wang and Carol Guion helped in the production, and their painstaking work is acknowledged with warm thanks.

Willis Harman
Richard Smoke

Introduction

This is a book on how to think about peace in a nuclear age. Peace now is not as precious as it has always been; it is *more* precious. The possible consequences of war have escalated to unthinkable dimensions. This small and fragile planet cannot afford a single global nuclear war. Hundreds of millions, possibly a billion or more, people would die in the first couple of hours. The whole species of humankind might be wiped out, along with many other species, in the environmental catastrophe, possibly including a "nuclear winter," that followed. The prevention of a global nuclear war is an absolute requirement if humanity is to have a future.

It is true that not every conflict could trigger a global nuclear war. But it is also true that no one is quite sure how to distinguish between those conflicts that might and those that won't. Some of the best-informed experts believe that the chance of war is significant. The requirement that there never be a global nuclear war, therefore, may not be easily achieved unless Albert Einstein's famous appeal for "new ways of thinking" is answered—by this generation and by generations to come.

Even though there have been many failures to maintain peace, the tone of this book is cautiously optimistic. It is important to know the limitations of old and new methods, but even more important to see the hope in the possibilities of their combination and in approaches not yet fully developed. The aim of the book is to help readers feel not only competent to hold opinions about what should be done but also motivated to make a contribution toward doing it.

What Is Peace?

The Romans had a saying, "If you desire peace, prepare for war." That maxim still guides the policies of the United States, the Soviet Union, and many other nations. In the nuclear age, we recommend that greater attention now be given to a different maxim, that of the

University for Peace, chartered by the United Nations and located in Costa Rica: "If you desire peace, educate for peace."

Peace, not just the avoidance of war, is important. It is both common sense and a profound psychological truth that people tend to create in reality the situations they imagine in their minds. If people focus on war, either looking forward to the victory or fearing the catastrophe, in subtle ways they may act to make war more probable. Even focusing on how to avoid a war may tend to postpone it rather than to transform the underlying conditions that give rise to it. Conversely, if people focus on peace, especially if they are realistic as well as imaginative in their thinking, they contribute toward peace. Thus thinking about peace is important, perhaps more so than is immediately apparent.

But thinking about peace is not as simple as it may seem. In the first place, the word itself is ambiguous. People who speak or write about peace often mean simply the absence of war. This "negative" definition conceives peace in terms of something else that is *not* happening, namely war. Less common but ultimately more satisfactory is a "positive" definition, one in terms of what *is* happening. This state of peace is one of harmony, mutual regard, and indeed active cooperation among the groups or nations involved—and ultimately the whole world.

Many who have intensively studied peace believe that a necessary accompaniment of this positive state is a sense of inner peace within at least many of the principal individuals leading these groups or nations. That state of inner serenity might be called "peace-*fullness*." Its absence is a subtle kind of psychological "emptiness" (which is really the beginning of feelings of insecurity).

Peace in the world is also a matter of degree. The fact that peace does not reign everywhere does not mean that it is not real in many places. Although some people are fighting with rifles as this book is being published, no one is fighting with nuclear missiles.

For our purposes in this book, it will be useful to define three peace goals, each representing a greater degree of peace. First, there is a long-term goal of what we will call *complete peace:* a sustainable state of nonviolence, and even low conflict, among peoples. Many assume that this is achievable only after nation-states have been replaced by some kind of world governance.

Second, there is a shorter-term goal that we will call *operational peace.* We will offer a more complete definition later, but for now we mean a reasonably universal conviction that war and weapons of mass destruction are no longer legitimate elements in international life and a reasonably consistent employment of peaceful means of conflict resolution among nations. This state is probably what most people imagine when they try to think realistically of how a peaceful world of the not-distant future might look.

The third goal is *abolishing the threat of a global nuclear holocaust.* This goal must be distinguished from operational peace, because various ways can be imagined in which the threat essentially be removed even though some warfare continued in some regions. In this book, we will be concerned mainly with the latter two goals. The first, complete peace, is a more distant ideal, the path to which can be best discerned when the other two goals have been achieved.

Nine Paths to Peace

This brief book presents nine basic ways in which people have tried, or might try, to achieve peace between nations. We examine and compare these ways, for they do not all apply to the same kinds of circumstances nor result in the same sorts of peace. The ninth is especially different from the others, for it does not pertain to governments or "policy." The nine are not mutually exclusive; indeed operational peace might well require the combined application of most or even all of them.

1. *Removing the source of the threat to peace.* Peace can sometimes be preserved by abolishing or taking away the conditions that are about to generate a war.

2. *Deterrence.* Peace of a kind can sometimes be preserved by threatening a potential enemy with unacceptable punishment if the enemy begins a war.

3. *Diplomacy for peace.* Classical diplomacy sometimes can, and sometimes has, preserved the peace.

4. *Disarmament and arms control.* One major source of war can be reduced or removed, and in principle any war rendered impossible, by reducing or removing the potential means of war.

5. *Eliminating the fundamental causes of war.* If the roots of war can be removed, no wars will erupt.

6. *Alternative defense.* Perhaps a quite different way of thinking about "defense" could produce methods that would discourage any aggressor more reliably and more safely than we can today.

7. *Nonviolent resistance.* Perhaps a civilian populace that is ready to engage in systematic nonviolence could also discourage any aggressor.

8. *Alternative conflict resolution.* New techniques might be developed for resolving conflicts among nations.

9. *Changing attitudes and perceptions.* A general change in the way people think about war and security could shift the framework in which international affairs proceed.

We believe virtually all major ideas about international peace fall into one of these nine categories or involve some combination of them. As we discuss these alternatives, we do so with the contemporary world situation in mind, especially the danger of nuclear war. But a historical perspective is helpful in assessing them: When were they used, and how successfully? What may have been learned?

Through a comparison of these nine paths we learn something about the relationship of one to another and also about the distinctive features, strengths, and weaknesses of each. In this book we also do two more things. We identify some of the especially significant *issues* that arise under each heading. (For example, can arms control and disarmament precede the political resolution of a conflict, or do they more successfully follow it?) And we identify some important *preconditions* for the success of each path. The feasibility of any of these approaches in any given situation depends on whether the distinctive preconditions are met.

The nine paths include very traditional ways of thinking about peace, such as deterrence and diplomacy, and also some unconventional concepts like nonviolence. The paths have been chosen to include both ways of coping with an ongoing or imminent conflict (that is, *achieving* peace when it does not exist now) and ways of preventing the emergence of conflict (that is, *maintaining* peace when it does exist). Table 1 should be useful now and as a reference while you continue reading.

TABLE 1
Nine Paths to Peace

	Traditional	Alternative
Coping with conflict	1. Removing the threat	6. Alternative defense
	2. Deterrence	7. Nonviolent resistance
Preventing conflict	3. Preventive diplomacy	8. Alternative conflict resolution
	4. Disarmament and arms control	9. Changing attitudes and perceptions
	5. Eliminating fundamental causes of conflict	

About This Book

The first four of the five chapters of this book follow this schema. Chapter 1 discusses the traditional means of coping with conflict: paths 1 and 2. Chapter 2 discusses the traditional means of trying to prevent conflict: paths 3, 4, and 5. The remaining chapters are largely devoted to new thinking. Chapter 3 takes up the alternative means of coping with conflict: paths 6 and 7. Chapter 4 goes on to the alternative means for preventing conflict: paths 8 and 9. Finally Chapter 5, "The Possibility of Peace," assesses humanity's contemporary situation more broadly, inquires into the real prospects for achieving operational peace or the abolition of the nuclear danger, and suggests some things that might be done to improve those prospects.

Naturally this book focuses mostly on what governments have done and might do, but it also speaks, especially in chapters 3, 4, and 5, to what "ordinary" people can do. It will be clear already that we, the authors, are not detached or antiseptically objective about peace and war and do not consider them merely as academic subjects. Peace matters. And attitudes about peace matter. We are convinced of this, and the bias will show. We believe that global nuclear war is a future that *must* be avoided and that bringing up generation after generation under the constant threat of possible nuclear holocaust is intolerable.

We also believe that humanity's chance of achieving peace on Earth may be greater now than at any time in recorded history. Chapter 4 and especially Chapter 5 lay out the reasons why we think so. We invite readers to consider for themselves the paths to peace and consider this conclusion for themselves as they examine our arguments. Many readers, we hope, will then go on to draw their own conclusions about the part they themselves might play in achieving peace.

1

Traditional Paths
to Coping with Conflict

Traditional ideas about coping with an existing or imminent conflict fall into two broad categories. One might take positive action to remove the threat, or one might tolerate the threat but prevent it from actually being carried out. In practice, the former involves some form of intervention, and the latter generally means *deterrence*. Let us look first at the former.

The Path of Removing the Threat

It might seem paradoxical to take action (often military action) to remove a threat to peace; in some applications this concept can indeed lead to situations that are paradoxical or contradictory. But to most people through the ages, and probably to a great many people today, removing the threat has often seemed the simple, sensible, and *moral* thing to do.

A classic example of a nation taking this path, apparently with success, was Israel's decision, in 1981, to destroy Iraq's Osirak nuclear reactor. Intelligence reports indicated that it was very possibly being used in a nuclear weapons program. Iraq had publicly stated that it planned to develop nuclear weapons and had rejected various international efforts to dissuade it from that course. Rather than risk Iraqi production of one or more bombs, the Israelis decided to remove the threat. At dawn on June 7, 1981, Israeli Air Force aircraft bombed and destroyed the reactor. Some guards at the site were killed, but casualties were light.

This action was a clear violation of Iraqi sovereignty and of various international laws, and most countries formally condemned it. But behind the formal condemnations, some governments and many people around the world quietly approved the Israeli action. The Iraqi government was generally seen by democratic nations as a tyrannical and irresponsible state—one that might actually use nuclear weapons. Many felt that the Israelis, by removing any imminent threat of an Iraqi atomic bomb, had acted not only in the Israeli interest but in the interest of peaceloving people everywhere. Scientists generally agreed afterward that the Israeli action had set back the Iraqi nuclear weapons program by several years at least, perhaps much longer.

That peace could be achieved by expunging a threat to peace has been such a popular and persuasive idea that it has been used as the main justification behind major wars. The U.S. entry into World War I is a classic example. President Woodrow Wilson was an idealist and a peaceloving man who abhorred war. For years he managed to keep the United States out of the European war. But repeated German submarine attacks on Allied shipping (including the sinking of the *Lusitania,* an unarmed British liner, with the loss of 128 American lives) and finally the attacks on U.S. merchant ships in March 1917 drove Wilson to the conclusion that the Kaiser's regime was an intolerable threat to the peace of the whole world. He convinced Congress to declare war against Germany substantially on those grounds. He announced to the people of the United States that U.S. military intervention would make this "a war to end war."

One may smile at the naiveté of this slogan in the light of the large number of wars that have occurred since. One may decide that Wilson's reasoning was casuistic or that his disappointed idealism led him into self-deception.[2] But there is no denying that large segments of the U.S. public felt that undertaking military action—in fact, entering a war—to eliminate the German threat to world peace was both a reasonable and a highly moral thing to do.

This moralistic attitude is characteristic of the United States, although it has been shared by many other peoples. Today, forty crisis-laden years since World War II, it is easy to forget that for two centuries previously, the United States had generally been unwilling to go to war without some such moral justification. At least until the time of the cold war with the Soviet Union, Americans thought of themselves as an unusually peaceful people and consistently refused, decade after decade, to support any large standing military establishment or any easy move toward war. The Spanish-American War of 1898 was justified in part because it removed a threat of war, and part of the U.S. motive in entering World War II was a conviction that the world could not be at peace until Hitler, Mussolini, and the Japanese warlords were removed from power.

There are many other examples of a policy of removing the threat being advocated or implemented in the name of restoring or achieving peace. On occasion the Roman Empire undertook a limited military action beyond its borders to nip some budding threat to the *pax Romana*. And in the late 1940s the British philosopher and pacifist Bertrand Russell recommended that the United States launch a preventive war against the Soviet Union. Russell, like Woodrow Wilson an unusually peaceloving man, feared the likelihood of nuclear war. He wanted the United States to forestall this threat by rendering the Soviet Union incapable of acquiring an arsenal of atomic weapons. He believed that a kind of *pax Americana*, backed by a continued U.S. monopoly of nuclear weapons, would be the best guarantee against the horror of nuclear war.

Preventive war, such as was advocated by Wilson and Russell, is the most extreme form of the basic concept of removing the threat as a path to peace. It is obviously the form that creates the greatest paradoxes and raises disturbing questions. A much milder variant is the single, quick action, such as the Israeli raid on the Osirak reactor. Still milder variants such as counterterrorist responses may be little more than police actions. In recent years a number of nations have formed commando or joint military/police teams that are able to raid terrorist cells, capture or kill airplane hijackers, and so on. One can imagine a spectrum of such removing-the-threat types of actions, ranging from counterterrorist actions at one end to the extreme of preventive war at the other.

To be successful, a variant of the remove-the-threat approach has to meet two kinds of preconditions—military-technical and moral-political. The Israelis, for example, had to satisfy certain military-technical preconditions if their Osirak raid was to succeed, and the details of the raid were arranged with great care. The raid might well have failed if either the Iraqi air defenses had been more effective or the Israeli Air Force less effective; the raid could not have been attempted a second time. The plan also had to meet some demanding moral-political conditions. The responsible Israeli government officials had to be satisfied not only that this course was feasible but also that it would be perceived as *right* by important "audiences." They had to satisfy themselves that a majority of the Israeli public would approve (which it did). Because Israel is highly dependent on U.S. support, they also had to be confident that the U.S. government and people would not object too seriously (as they didn't).

In general, moral-political conditions become more difficult to meet as the intensity of the action increases. As actions move toward the extreme end of the spectrum mentioned previously, public support generally declines, and the severity of the moral ambiguities and paradoxes increases. Hardly anyone disapproves if a police team, raiding a cell where explosives are being prepared, finds it necessary to kill a few terrorists. The case for a preventive war is harder to make. The questions become far more troubling: Is this action justifiable to the world? How problematic is the expected positive outcome? How great will the costs really be, in casualties and matériel? Will the action set a bad example for other countries? Would not the world be in a worse situation if everyone started behaving this way? Doesn't this action violate principles of peace and justice, even if the short-term cost/benefit ratio may seem favorable? It may be that questions like these have been asked more insistently as we moved further into the anxious era in which we now live. Russell's suggestion was never seriously considered in Washington, and years later searching moral questions were asked during and after the U.S. Vietnamese adventure.

It may seem unlikely that the United States would deliberately undertake a preemptive remove-the-threat strike that could start a major war. However, such decisions sometimes come at the end of a chain of actions that were not intended to bring about such a catastrophic consequence. Certainly many people fear that in some future crisis a superpower might be tempted to make a preemptive strike somewhat as Japan did on Pearl Harbor in 1941. Obviously this would be the most extreme and most self-destructive misuse of the removing-the-threat idea in humanity's history.

Whether far more moderate actions to remove threats to peace in the future might be justified, at least in some circumstances, will probably remain debatable for a long time to come. Certainly in the 1980s, this path sometimes has the support of the majority of people.

The Path of Deterrence

When it has not seemed reasonable to take action to remove a serious threat because of practical or moral or political considerations, nations have often attempted to deter the menacing nation from carrying out the threatening action. For decades deterrence has been the official policy of both the United States and the Soviet Union with regard to nuclear weapons. Deterrence has become a household word, and the basic idea is widely understood. Deterrence is a contingent threat: "If you attack me, I shall retaliate by attacking you." The implicit promise is "If you do not attack me, I will not attack you." The basic deterrent threat made by each of the superpowers is to destroy the other with nuclear weapons should the other launch a major nuclear attack.

Although its entry into the common vocabulary is recent, deterrence is a very old idea. For example, the Roman Empire often succeeded in preventing attack from outside its borders by threatening a retaliatory invasion. The empire could not possibly keep every section of its long frontier strongly defended, and thus it might have been relatively easy for an invading tribe or kingdom to penetrate the border and even temporarily occupy some Roman territory. But it was well understood that eventually Rome would gather its legions, push back and defeat the invader, and very likely occupy the invader's land or administer severe punishment. Thus the empire was often not attacked because potential enemies understood that the price would be intolerably high for the offending nation. Rome fell not when its borders became weak (they were always weak), but when its central power declined to the point that the threat of devastating counterattack was no longer convincing, that is, the deterrent threat was no longer credible.

Until recent times deterrence was not treated as policy separate from the capacity to defeat the enemy, because both were essentially the same thing: The capacity to defeat the attacking army *was* the deterrent threat. The same situation continues today among nations with powerful military forces but without nuclear weapons. India and Pakistan, for instance, are mutually hostile and have fought three wars since the two countries were formed in 1947. Neither is eager to start a fourth war because both have learned that their forces are evenly enough matched that the costs of another war are likely to outweigh any conceivable gains. (Some experts expect this situation may change.)

Deterrence became an identified policy, differentiated from the capability to defeat enemy forces, around the middle of the twentieth century. The development of nuclear weapons and of bombers and missiles for long-range delivery created a separation between the capacity to defeat and the capacity to deter. It was no longer necessary to defeat the enemy's military forces before one could inflict massive punishing damage. The threat could be plausibly made that within hours or even minutes of a military attack, bombers and missiles would inflict intolerably severe destruction on the aggressor's homeland. Punishment became effectively disconnected from military "victory" and "defeat" in the traditional sense of the terms.

There are two important preconditions for a policy of deterrence to be separately identifiable from military defense. One is that the punishment threatened must be very great—clearly and unquestionably greater than the potential aggressor nation might be prepared to bear. Nuclear weapons are so hideously destructive that they are extremely well suited to this criterion. The other precondition is that there can be no effective defense against the threat. (And it is necessary that both the deterrer and the deterred *know* that there is no effective defense.) It is clear that no effective defense has yet been developed against long-range ballistic missiles with nuclear warheads. If a defense against the punishment existed, then obviously the threat would not be so meaningful. It is precisely because nations are so utterly vulnerable to nuclear attack and because attack could be so overwhelmingly devastating that deterrence has assumed a unique place in contemporary international relations.

Deterrence as a means of keeping peace is extremely sensitive to technological advance. For example, if advancing technology can provide an effective defense, then nuclear deterrence might no longer be a viable approach to achieving peace.

When President Reagan put forth his policy-reversing Strategic Defense Initiative (SDI or "Star Wars") in March 1983, it was promoted as a substitution of defense for deterrence—a way of "rising above dealing with other nations and human beings by threatening their existence." Once scientists had developed an infallible way of intercepting and destroying strategic missiles, "no longer would our countrymen have to rely on retaliation to protect them from nuclear attack." However, most scientists doubt that effective defense of civilian populations against nuclear attack is a possibility in the foreseeable future. Even the two study teams that the president asked to report to him later that year, one on Defensive Technology and the other on Future Security Strategies, questioned the feasibility of a "nuclear umbrella." The latter argued that it might be possible to safeguard land-based missile silos and other military targets but not the entire U.S. population. Protecting silos, the report said, would result in "strengthening deterrence" because such limited-objective defense measures could "deny Soviet planners confidence in their ability to destroy a sufficient set of military targets to satisfy enemy attack objectives." Arms negotiator Paul Nitze has defended the SDI as "wholly consistent with deterrence."

"Star Wars," then, comprises two programs and two goals under a single name. Whether or not President Reagan's "dream" (as he called it) of a defense of populations might be achievable someday, many national security specialists fear that any development and deployment of silo defenses that undercut the ABM Treaty, coupled (perhaps) with primitive, inadequate population defenses, could trigger a massive all-out arms race between the U.S. and the USSR.

Nuclear deterrence, unlike the historically common deterrence by superior military power, rests on a logical paradox. Jonathan Schell pointed this out in his provocative book *The Fate of the Earth*, as have many other writers. It is, they say, essentially a bluff. For if the Soviet Union ever did launch a massive nuclear attack on the United States, decimating the population and destroying the cities, why should the United States actually destroy the Soviet Union in return? At that point the deterrent threat would have failed, so it would be pointless to carry it out. The basic flaw in nuclear deterrence, these critics say, is that there would be no reason to carry out the deed once the threat had failed. Proponents of nuclear deterrence acknowledge the logical paradox, but reply that no nation's leaders would ever dare count on the leaders of the destroyed country reasoning so abstractly; there is a great risk that the surviving leaders of the destroyed country would retaliate out of sheer vengeance.

Logical and psychological considerations aside, many people are troubled by the moral implications of nuclear deterrence. How can it be right to threaten the sudden death of hundreds of millions of human beings, no matter what the reason? How can it be right to create and put in place the armaments for actually doing this, knowing that they might be used some day, perhaps even unintentionally? Reliance on the nuclear balance of terror to preserve "peace" involves a continuing threat to engage in terrorism on the largest imaginable scale. It seems to violate a basic precept of the international law, reaffirmed at the Nuremberg trials, prohibiting reliance on weapons and tactics of indiscriminate destruction.

On such moral grounds some people reject nuclear deterrence altogether. Its proponents, however, respond that the overwhelming threat will never actually be carried out; the tens of millions of deaths are purely hypothetical. The whole point of deterrence is to *prevent* either side from using nuclear weapons. They add that no nuclear wars have ever been fought and that the nuclear-armed nations have demonstrated great caution in their relations with each other.

A third, intermediate position has been advanced by Pope John Paul II, by the American Catholic Bishops, and by a number of others. In this view nuclear deterrence is morally tolerable as long as it is temporary—a way to maintain "a sort of peace" while energetic efforts are made to move beyond it. However it is not morally tolerable if it exists indefinitely or permanently.

As this all suggests, the most serious argument against deterrence is that the condition it creates is not really peace. Nuclear deterrence is costly, and it carries terrible risks. Just as removing the threat often involves an internal contradiction, so deterrence as a way of achieving "peace" involves the contradiction that while the situation created is not war, it is not stable peace either. Deterrence may not require actual fighting or destruction. But for the deterring threat to be credible, the threatener must be constantly ready to fight. Furthermore, this state may have to go on for a long time (as contrasted with removing the threat by a single decisive preemptive action).

This objection to deterrence is not just an intellectual or even a moral one. Psychologists are discovering that a perpetual state of nuclear deterrence has emotional consequences, perhaps especially for children. A number of studies have indicated that a significant percentage of children in the United States have recurring nightmares and/or waking anxieties that they may or may not be able to express. It seems likely that adults also have similar fears, more deeply buried. Deterrence is fundamentally based on fear (its root word is the same as for the word "terror"), and deterrence with nuclear weapons is based on fear of awesome destruction. It is a perversion of the meaning of the word to call such a psychological climate "peace."

However, the profound and special problems associated with *nuclear* deterrence should not be allowed to obscure the fact that, in the broadest sense of the term, deterrence is inescapably a part of many aspects of human life. Police walk the streets in order to deter thugs from open assault. Jails are meant to deter potential criminals. Parents regularly deter children from misbehavior by the threat of punishment.

Deterrence in more subtle forms is a part of most collective behavior. For instance, labor unions deter management from exploiting the workers by explicit or implicit threat of a strike; management in turn deters labor from making excessive demands by the threat of plant shutdown or the possibility of going out of business. In international relations, governments may deter other governments from taking unwanted actions by threat of economic sanctions such as trade reduction; subtle deterrence is ever-present in international diplomacy. For example, after New Zealand decided in February 1985 to deny port visiting rights to U.S. naval vessels that might be carrying nuclear weapons, senior U.S. officials said that "to deter other allied countries from following New Zealand's example" the United States was considering various retaliations, including ending preferential treatment in the U.S. market for New Zealand lamb.[3]

Deterrence in all its forms is essentially a psychological process. What makes it effective is the credibility of the threat. If the party being threatened believes that the threat is real, then he or she will be deterred; it does not matter whether the threatener is in fact able or willing to carry out the threat. Conversely, if the threatened party does *not* believe the threat to be real, the threat will not deter, even if the threatener is in fact prepared to carry out the threat. (The threatener may be forced to carry it out, but in this case the threatener gains credibility only after deterrence has failed.) In deterrence, belief is everything. This is true whether the threat be that the Soviet Union will be annihilated or that the child will be spanked.

Deterrence also requires accurate communication of what behavior the threatener wishes to forbid. Even if the threatened party believes that the punishment will indeed be inflicted, he or she may not be deterred if it is not clear what action would trigger the punishment. It is easy to imagine that as a result of misunderstandings between different cultures or a breakdown in communications between nations, two parties could have different perceptions of what is forbidden.

Credibility and communication, then, are essential for successful deterrence. Because both can be problematic, social scientists have studied what conditions tend to add to or detract from credibility in various situations and how communication can maximize the deterrent effect. (For example, a degree of deliberate ambiguity may be useful: The teenager told he'll lose the privilege of driving the family car if he is out "too late" may come home earlier than if he is told an exact hour.)

All of the alternate paths to peace discussed in later chapters involve deterrence in significant ways. The path of nonviolence, for instance, inherently involves a form of deterrence. Mahatma Gandhi employed deterrence regularly by implicitly (occasionally explicitly) threatening the British with mass demonstrations if they took repressive action against the movement toward Indian independence.

Deterrence in some form is likely to be a part of any political or international situation. In the commonest use of the word today, deterrence refers to the threat of nuclear destruction or effective military action (as in the example of India and Pakistan). But deterrence has many other meanings, and the moral significance and psychological impact vary tremendously, depending on the nature of the threat. For example, Gandhi's threats to the British did not involve killing; his main threat was to make the British look foolish in the eyes of the world and ultimately in their own eyes. It is essential to ask of any use of deterrence, "What is the threat being made?"

Summary

The traditional paths to coping with an existing or imminent threat to peace involve taking direct action to remove the threat and/or deterring conflict with a threat of retaliation or punishment. Normally one would expect to remove an existing threat and to deter an imminent threat. But one may also take action to remove a seemingly imminent danger, as the Israelis did with the Osirak reactor. And one may seek to deter an existing low-level threat from escalating to a higher level.

There is paradox involved both with action to remove a threat and with the threat of punishment to deter a threat, insofar as they are viewed as paths to peace. Both require some measure of violence, actual or threatened, to reach the desired goal of peace. How morally tolerable, and how politically feasible, this violence will be depends upon many factors and may involve complex and difficult questions. Thoughtful individuals, committed to behaving as ethically as possible, can come to quite different judgments.

2

Traditional Paths
to Preventing Conflict

When and where peace exists, the task is to maintain it. There are three traditional paths to this goal:

First, there can be efforts to reduce a nation's *incentive* to begin planning a military aggression. These have usually focused on reducing the need to gain something that might be achievable by war, on modifying the circumstances so that a war would be pointless, and on facilitating negotiations among disputing nations. The most common name for such efforts is preventive diplomacy.

Second, there can be efforts to reduce or eliminate the *means* by which nations might make war. Although most often these attempts have focused on reducing or eliminating categories of weapons, they have sometimes included proposals to reduce the numbers of military personnel or to change the locations where military forces are positioned. Today these efforts are usually called arms control and disarmament.

Third, there can be efforts to remove the *deeper roots* of war. On the assumption that there are underlying causes of war that are ultimately more important than the immediate reasons for which a nation might go to war, this approach seeks to identify those causes and remove, or at least mitigate, them. In this chapter we shall look at each of these three paths in turn.

The Path of Preventive Diplomacy

Diplomacy has many possible goals, of which peace is only one. For instance a nation may, through diplomacy, seek to improve its position in the world or attain some specific objectives. The result may be something as tangible as the U.S. purchase of Alaska from Russia in the 1860s or as intangible as the gain in international prestige that Malta achieved by championing the Law of the Sea Treaty in the 1970s.

Diplomacy aimed at improving one's position or attaining specific objectives may not be benign. A nation may, for instance, try a diplomacy of intimidation. Hitler did so repeatedly, and in the main successfully, in the late 1930s. The Soviet Union's attempt to intimidate West Germany in 1983, when the Germans were considering whether to accept new land-based U.S. missiles, was less successful. Of course, a diplomacy of intimidation is not necessarily limited to dictatorships. Several times in the early 1980s the United States sent aircraft carriers to Central American waters and conducted major troop exercises in Central America—actions intended partly to intimidate the Nicaraguan government and leftist insurgents elsewhere in Central America.

Of all the possible goals of diplomacy, a major one for many nations much of the time—and the one we are concerned with here—is the prevention of war. It is useful to distinguish between two varieties of preventive diplomacy. One type involves *unilateral diplomacy* by a single nation (or an alliance of nations acting together). The other kind involves the creation of *multilateral mechanisms*—collective international organizations such as the United Nations, regional groupings like the Organization of American States (OAS), agreements on international law, and so forth.

The simplest kind of unilateral diplomacy for peace is the sort of activity at which Sweden and Switzerland have proven to be especially proficient—namely, assisting in diplomatic processes that can help maintain peace. This assistance may include hosting and defraying the costs of international conferences, providing staff and other support for these conferences, acting as neutral arbiter, and so on. Sweden transfers an unusually high percentage of its diplomatic personnel to the United Nations and international agencies, and Switzerland provides land and facilities in Geneva for a tremendous range of diplomatic activities.

Both countries declare that peace is the chief goal of their diplomacy. Both are neutral and are advantageously poised between two roughly equal power blocs. (Canada and Finland, which might like to play a similar role, are less well placed geographically.) Neutral countries in this "middle" position equate their own national security with the maintenance of peace. They would likely be overrun and destroyed regardless of who started a major war or how or why it was started. (In addition to their diplomatic efforts, both Sweden and Switzerland also maintain modern, expensive, powerfully armed forces, configured to be able to defend but not attack.)

A nation that is not between two opposing forces, but rather is one (or part of one) of the opposing forces, is in a different position. India and Pakistan, Syria and Israel, Greece and Turkey, the U.S. and the USSR are pairs of opposing nations. For them, national security may also require peace, but in a slightly different sense. For them, unilateral preventive diplomacy has a different meaning.

These nations too say, often sincerely, that peace is the chief goal of their diplomacy, but the significance of their claim is different from that of a similar pronouncement by Sweden or Switzerland. Nations (or alliances) in a mutually hostile relationship with another nation generally see the other, not themselves, as the probable source of war. Hence their preventive diplomacy is aimed primarily at preventing the other side (rather than themselves or the system as a whole) from moving toward war. This might be called *adversarial* preventive diplomacy. It usually aims at creating circumstances in which the other side will not want to move toward war.

An example of adversarial preventive diplomacy on the grandest scale is provided by the U.S. policy, in the second half of the twentieth century, of *containment* of the Soviet Union. At its peak this policy marshaled fifty-five nations into five distinct alliance systems that were in addition to bilateral alliance agreements. Containment has, as of this writing, been a fundamental principle of U.S. diplomacy for two generations (nearly forty years).

Containment begins by taking seriously the Soviet claim that communism, as defined by Moscow, will eventually sweep the world. The Soviet claim emphasizes the Leninist principles of attaining this objective by deliberate action and by all effective means rather than the Marxist principle of "historical inevitability." The containment policy identifies the Soviet Union as the source of expected aggressive actions and sets the fundamental goal of frustrating those actions. In this view, the impulse toward communism is seen as originating in one center, Moscow, and radiating outward (rather than as originating in many places). It is this impulse that must be contained.

In its attempt to stem the communist threat, the United States created an enormous panoply of means—political, diplomatic, military, economic—and orchestrated them over decades in a tremendous display of adversarial preventive diplomacy (simultaneous with the policy of deterring nuclear attack). Symmetrically identifying the capitalist United States as the source of threat, the USSR practiced a similar preventive diplomacy on a lesser scale. Each country, working within its basic assumptions about the nature of peace and justice, was sincere in declaring that its preventive diplomacy was intended to maintain peace in the world.

Even if one concludes that each of these particular efforts is deluded in greater or lesser degree, it does not follow that adversarial preventive diplomacy is always a mistake. Many scholars now believe that a strong preventive diplomacy of this kind, carried out by Britain, France, and the USSR in the 1930s, could have successfully contained Hitler's Germany and either prevented or made less costly a new European war.

In addition to the kind of functional diplomacy typified by Sweden and Switzerland and the adversarial preventive diplomacy illustrated in the U.S.-USSR example, there is a third kind of unilateral preventive diplomacy. A nation that has a mild dispute with another nation may decide that maintaining peaceful and good relations is too important to allow the dispute to escalate into serious conflict and so may find a peaceful resolution. Almost invariably, two preconditions must exist before such a decision can be reached. One condition is that the dispute does not involve the nation's security in any major way. The other condition is that the dispute is seen as a single, isolated matter. Only then can one nation back down without the fear that doing so will lead to new demands from the other side.

Disputes between nations may also be resolved without armed conflict by using collective mechanisms already in place. Mechanisms like the UN, the OAS, and international law exist for two main reasons. One reason is to carry out functional purposes. The UN, for instance, supports a number of international bodies like the World Health Organization (which coordinates medical relief, works to prevent epidemics, and so forth) and the International Telecommunications Union (which assigns bands on the radio and television frequency spectrum, coordinates use of communication satellites, and so on). These and other functional agencies work to carry out global purposes that no nation or small group of nations could accomplish alone. Similarly, the OAS and other regional groupings coordinate trade within their regions. International law regulates all these kinds of activities and is routinely referred to, often without serious dispute, as a guideline for conduct in trade, telecommunications, and other matters.

The second rationale for the existence of the UN, regional groupings, and some parts of international law is to carry out preventive diplomacy. One of the key institutions of the UN, the Security Council, was designed to prevent war by its capacity to marshal most of the world in opposition to any potential new aggressor. But the veto provision, which allowed action to be blocked by any one of the permanent members, together with the cold war division of the world into two hostile camps, rendered the council almost completely ineffective in this role. (The UN General Assembly has played an important substitute role, however.) The secretary-general of the UN and several regional organizations have served as mediators when two nations have sought outside assistance to resolve a dispute. And the International Court of Justice has adjudicated disputes in which two contending parties have turned to international law. (Strictly speaking, the operation of the court is not usually regarded as preventive diplomacy; however, the creation of and the decision to use the court would be so regarded.)

We cannot discuss all the various collective mechanisms for maintaining peace that have been tried (let alone proposed). In the present era, three types are probably of greatest interest.

Collective sanctions have often been proposed, and sometimes tried, as a warning to nations that have broken the peace (or seem likely to). For example, the League of Nations attempted to organize an economic embargo against Italy after Mussolini invaded Ethiopia in 1935. The effort did not damage Italy seriously and was eventually abandoned. A similar attempt against South Africa, organized by the UN General Assembly in the late 1970s, had also not succeeded by 1986, although the effort continued and showed signs of becoming more economically significant in the future. (This embargo was primarily intended to change South Africa's racial policies. The possibility that the country would resort to war to defend its social system was a subsidiary rationale; the case was made that Pretoria was already "at war" against the majority of its own population.)

Mediation can succeed when there is a genuine desire on the part of the nations involved to see their dispute ended. Most often, the conflicts successfully mediated are ones that would probably not have led to war anyway, but there are a few exceptions. In the early 1980s, mediation by the Vatican successfully resolved a long-standing border dispute between Chile and Argentina, a dispute that had at times seemed grave enough to cause war.

Peacekeeping forces have proven highly successful under some circumstances. Ten times between 1955 and 1985, peacekeeping forces created by the UN General Assembly or by the secretary-general with subsequent General Assembly approval helped to prevent a conflict from erupting into fighting—in Kashmir, southern Africa, Cyprus, and various points in the Middle East. Peacekeeping forces function primarily by separating the potential combatants, and placing neutral forces between them. These forces also make clear who is responsible if fighting resumes because the report of the UN forces will be generally believed. The opprobrium for making war on neutral peacekeepers is so great that a nation contemplating a war must first have the peacekeepers withdrawn; for example, Nasser insisted in 1967 that the UN peacekeeping forces in the Sinai be withdrawn. (Nasser in this case was bluffing; he hoped to pressure Israel into making concessions by seeming to threaten war.)

Agreement between potential adversaries to limit competition is another kind of preventive diplomacy. Although this type of diplomacy is multilateral, it does not involve (or only secondarily involves) the kinds of mechanisms that we usually think of as being part of collective security. In contemporary times, the best example of such agreements is a set of largely unwritten understandings that the United States and the Soviet Union have reached to try to keep their competition under control. Both sides understand, for instance, the importance of preventing situations in which U.S. and Soviet troops clash with each other directly. In 1972 the two superpowers also signed an agreement, which has proven partially successful, intended to keep a safe separation between their naval units.

The Americans and Soviets have also worked out, by trial and error rather than by formal agreement, an approach to conflicts in the Third World that involves an element of preventive diplomacy. The superpowers compete for influence in such areas as the Middle East and in several Middle Eastern wars have backed their respective dependents with quick transfusions of fresh military equipment; but the U.S. and the USSR try to keep these regional conflicts from becoming too severe. And when war breaks out, leaders in Washington and Moscow negotiate to limit their interventions so that the chances are reduced of the conflict escalating into a grave superpower crisis. Clearly this kind of limited approach to mutual preventive diplomacy allows the perpetuation of many risks of a major war. It may also encourage local conflicts even while constraining them. Even so, this approach creates a better situation than the one that might exist if the Americans and Soviets made no such efforts at all.

A more developed form of this kind of preventive diplomacy existed in the nineteenth century and for some decades was highly effective. Created at the Congress of Vienna in 1815, held after Napoleon was vanquished, this system came to be called the Concert of Europe. It lasted through most of the century but was most effective prior to 1850. Under this system, a nation that had lost something or seen a rival gain something would receive some form of "compensation" agreed upon by the "great powers." This device allowed tensions to be siphoned off rather than accumulated. Still more important, the Concert of Europe included a general understanding that, should a crisis erupt, the European nations would call a congress, to be attended not only by the nations involved but also by their neighbors and important neutrals. The congress would convene before nations resorted to war and would strive to achieve a negotiated solution that would make war unnecessary.

The Concert system did not always succeed, and several important wars were fought in Europe during the nineteenth century (notably in 1852, 1859, 1867, and 1870). But all of these were small in terms of costs and casualties, compared to the great wars that preceded and followed the Concert system—namely, the Napoleonic Wars and World War I. Through most of the century Europe was entirely at peace.

At least five conditions made the Concert system possible. Four of them could not be reproduced today; one condition that might be duplicated is the relatively even balance of power among the great powers of the day. In those days, countries had to take many weeks to mobilize their armies. The congress had time to meet. Today nations keep their military forces mobilized constantly or can mobilize very quickly. Also most of the great powers involved in the Concert were imperialist. Thus the aggressive impulses that they curbed in Europe could be carried abroad and exercised in what we now call the Third World. There was also a common understanding among all the great powers about the significance of current history and about how the future should develop. Just the opposite applies to today's two superpowers. Finally, the decisionmakers of the European nations were drawn largely from a single social class, the nobility, members of which intermarried across national boundaries and felt a greater interest in the perpetuation of the system than in the gain of advantage for one nation.

Preventive diplomacy, in summary, is a path to peace that involves a number of diverse techniques. It can be attempted unilaterally by nations having mild disputes that they are willing to resolve through negotiated agreement or by nations feeling serious threats from powerful adversaries. Preventive diplomacy can also be attempted multilaterally and can involve the creation of collective mechanisms to provide mediation or impose sanctions or position peacekeeping forces.

It is impossible to be sure how often preventive diplomacy has succeeded in preventing war for the same reason that it is impossible to determine how often deterrence has done so: One can never know whether war would really have occurred in the absence of the preventive measures. Experts' best judgment is that preventive diplomacy succeeds often enough to make imaginative efforts to extend it and employ it well worthwhile.

The Path of Disarmament and Arms Control

Preventive diplomacy tries to reduce the incentive to move toward war that national decisionmakers may feel; the path of disarmament and arms control tries to reduce the *means* by which they might make war. The distinction is not absolute because the means available do affect incentives. Decisionmakers who feel that they have adequate means to carry out a war successfully will probably have a stronger incentive to launch an ambitious war, and decisionmakers who fear a potential enemy's growing means may consider launching a preventive war.

Still, the distinction is a useful one. Advocates of disarmament and arms control have often thought the attempt to eliminate or reduce the means of warfare worthwhile because it seems a simpler approach than trying to eliminate all the many complex incentives to war that may exist. Complete and lasting disarmament of all nations would be the ultimate goal of this approach because such a condition would presumably make war impossible. But this ideal has seemed so out of reach that no serious effort to achieve it has ever been made. Instead, a number of lesser goals have been advanced, and from time to time temporarily or partially achieved.

One goal, minor compared to the general goal of preserving peace but still important, has been to abolish certain especially horrible weapons. For instance, the terrible experience with poison gas on the battlefields during World War I led to the Geneva Protocol in 1925, an agreement outlawing the use—though not the possession—of chemical weapons. (Curiously, the United States, which took the initiative in creating the protocol, declined afterward to ratify it, finally doing so only in 1974.) Poison gas was not used in World War II or in any other war since. (The Iran-Iraq War is a probable exception.) The major warring nations in World War II were mutually deterred from chemical warfare partly because each knew that the others had stockpiled chemical weapons. But the power of the Geneva Protocol was a contributing reason for the forbearance, and the protocol is still seen as the embodiment of an international consensus that the use of poison gas in war is intolerable. The outlawing of dum-dum bullets (bullets with soft tops that expand and shatter in the body) is another example of the abolition of especially horrible weapons by mutual agreement.

Some people have advocated abolishing nuclear weapons on the same grounds.

Another, related goal of disarmament has been the abolition of weapons that are dangerous to all parties. The argument is made that everyone should agree to abolish weapons that are potentially as dangerous for the user as for the victim. The main example to date has been biological weapons. A new disease strain, deliberately dispersed among enemy troops and/or population, is too likely to spread to one's own population, and advance inoculation of one's entire population would probably be both infeasible and provocative. The United States unilaterally renounced biological war and preparations for it in 1969, and in 1972 the U.S. and the Soviet Union signed a Biological Weapons Convention that forbids biological weapons. Although some questions have been raised about compliance, this convention is often mentioned as an important disarmament success.

It has been proposed that nuclear weapons be abolished or at least greatly reduced in number, on grounds that they are too dangerous. The most recent and powerful form of this argument is promulgated around the concept of the "nuclear winter." Mathematical models of the atmosphere have suggested that the large quantities of dust and smoke (from burning cities and forests) that would be produced by the explosion of many nuclear weapons could spread around the planet in the upper atmosphere, producing cold and darkness that might last for months. The climate change could cause massive extinction of life forms. If these models are correct, the use of nuclear weapons in quantity would be highly dangerous to the user even if the victim did not retaliate. Recent research, however, casts some doubt on the validity of the models.

Attempts to reduce or limit nations' major armaments have been made with two other goals in mind. One goal is halting or limiting the arms race: Arms races between countries absorb resources that would be better used for constructive purposes and add to tensions that might eventually erupt in war. A second goal is to limit the death and destruction if war does occur. The goals of halting or limiting arms races and of lessening the consequences of war have been sought through arms control by the world's great powers before World War I, between the two world wars, and again in the decades since World War II. There have also been some similar efforts (not discussed here) at a regional level—among Latin American nations, for example.

At the end of the nineteenth century, when the Concert of Europe system was beginning to break down, attention turned to arms control as a means of preserving the peace. The great powers of Europe were competing with each other in the size and power of their armies and navies, and tensions were rising. In 1899 and again in 1907, peace conferences were held at The Hague in the Netherlands. Arms reductions were on the agenda of the first conference and were proposed for the agenda of the second, but the subject was not addressed at either conference. Various countries' suspicions of each other's motives and fears of being locked into inferior positions prevented any serious consideration of the issue.

Navies were a special problem. During the decade before the outbreak of World War I, Germany and Great Britain competed in a threatening and increasingly tense race to build large warships ("capital ships"). The governments in London and Berlin repeatedly proposed agreements—to put ceilings on the two naval programs, to postpone construction, and otherwise to limit their naval competition. All the proposals failed. Some were attached to political conditions that the other side found unacceptable; others failed because they did not grant the opposite side as strong a position. The naval arms race directly contributed to the growing hostility between Britain and Germany. (However, the eventual war had many other contributing causes and was triggered by a whole chain of misunderstandings and miscalculations.)

At the close of World War I the victors imposed drastic arms limitations on the defeated nations but were reluctant to limit their own military power. Serious consideration of disarmament was delayed when it was made the responsibility of the new League of Nations organization, and no general negotiations took place until 1932, when a World Disarmament Conference began. It seemed to be making real progress on defining low armaments levels that the major powers could agree on. But Adolf Hitler came to power in January 1933 and in October withdrew Germany from the conference. No further arms control was possible before World War II.

Navies were an exception to the failure of arms control in the period between the wars. Although no general disarmament could be achieved, agreements were reached on limiting large warships— agreements that were adhered to for a short time by the major naval powers. At the first conference on this subject, held in Washington, D.C., in 1922, the U.S. secretary of state stunned the negotiators by making public the U.S. position at a time when everyone expected the negotiations to remain secret. The United States proposed the establishment of fixed ratios in capital ships among the five leading navies of the world. The public in North America and Europe, appalled at the mayhem caused by World War I, were eager for any progress toward permanent peace and enthusiastically supported the U.S. proposal. Under this public pressure, the negotiators felt compelled to agree. Slightly modified agreements were reaffirmed at a followup conference in London in 1930. But Japan withdrew from the agreements in 1934, and a third conference in 1935 weakened them further. Naval competition was already increasing in the categories of ships that the agreements did not cover, and by the late 1930s the agreements were essentially null.

Another response to the post-World War I public revulsion to war was one of the most ambitious peace plans ever put forward. The Kellogg-Briand Pact of 1928 was signed by sixty-two nations, including all of the major powers. It was not exactly a disarmament plan but rather a multilateral agreement to renounce war as an instrument of national policy and to settle all international disputes by peaceful means. The signatories allowed themselves a variety of qualifications and interpretations, however. The pact did not prohibit wars of self-defense or military obligations arising from the League of Nations Covenant, the Monroe Doctrine, or postwar treaties of alliance. These qualifications, plus the fact that the treaty did not provide for sanctions against offenders, combined to make the Kellogg-Briand Pact ineffective. (It did play an important role later, however, as one of the legal bases of the Nuremberg trials.)

Since World War II, almost all attention to arms control has focused on controlling nuclear arms. Exceptions include the Biological Weapons Convention of 1972 and some continuing but unproductive work on further chemical weapons controls. Nuclear weapons are so potentially devastating that everyone agrees that any serious control of arms must deal with the nuclear issue.

Just after World War II, the United States, which then had a monopoly of nuclear weapons, put forth the "Baruch Plan," which proposed the transfer of all control of nuclear research and facilities to an international policing body linked to the UN. Weapons research would be forbidden, and the U.S. would give up its weapons. The plan would, however, have left the United States as sole possessor of the knowledge of how to construct nuclear weapons; no other country could acquire it under the proposed regime. For this reason and others, the Soviet Union rejected the plan. The USSR then produced its own plan, under which the UN Security Council would control enforcement; the USSR in turn could veto any actions taken by the council. Serious negotiations soon ceased.

During the 1950s, various schemes for partial nuclear disarmament were discussed, but they fell afoul of mutual suspicion, of Soviet efforts to split the Western allies, of Western desire for superiority, and of advancing technology. Disillusionment with partial schemes led briefly to plans, offered by both sides, for complete and general disarmament—that is, the *total* dismantling of the major powers' military forces. But these schemes were not taken seriously and probably were not intended to be.

In the 1960s the approach changed. Experts and governments shifted their attention from trying to halt the arms race to trying to channel and control it. The term *arms control* came into vogue. Since then full disarmament has rarely been discussed seriously.

Soon some significant successes resulted from the arms control approach. The most successful agreements were the 1963 Limited Test Ban Treaty, which ended worldwide fallout from open-air nuclear testing, and the 1968 Non-Proliferation Treaty, which severely limited what otherwise might have been a rapid spread of nuclear weapons into the hands of more and more nations. Other agreements closed off Latin America (1967), the seabed (1971), and, in part, outer space (1967) as territories in the nuclear arms race.

The most elaborate arms control effort ever attempted came in the 1970s with the Strategic Arms Limitation Talks (SALT). Although the ABM Treaty forbade defenses against ballistic missiles and therefore presumably reduced either side's need to build more of these missiles, both sides continued to build. In effect, the SALT agreements on offensive arms merely ratified these buildups; the numbers agreed upon were juggled to permit each side to carry out further planned deployments.

Talks in the early 1980s about both strategic and European nuclear issues began from viewpoints so far apart that they predictably accomplished nothing. In 1985 negotiations were complicated by the U.S. insistence on pursuing its "Star Wars" initiative, which reopened the question of defenses against missiles. As of this writing in 1986, prospects for significant additional control of nuclear arms in the near future appear dim—*unless*, as happened in the 1920s, sufficient *public pressure* develops to force the negotiating governments into more action.

What is one to make of the record of disarmament and arms control efforts? How successful has this path to peace been, and how successful can it be?

The effort since World War II to control nuclear arms has at least succeeded in halting worldwide fallout from atmospheric testing and in slowing considerably the proliferation of nuclear weapons—two important accomplishments. It also banned missile defenses. There have been some minor successes as well. But the nuclear arms control effort has also developed important *disadvantages* as a method of preserving peace—and even as a way to stop arms races and reduce the consequences of war.

One disadvantage resulted from the shift in objective, during the 1960s, from halting to channeling the nuclear arms race. The net effect, as institutionalized in SALT, was to negotiate and sanction buildups in offensive weapons under the rubric of "arms control." These buildups were somewhat constrained; nevertheless a dozen years after SALT began, the U.S. and the USSR had each increased by five times their arsenals of strategic nuclear warheads, and each had more weapon delivery systems. Widespread public support for a complete "freeze" on building offensive warheads and delivery systems, evidenced in the early 1980s, was not successfully translated into arms control policy or into an agreement.

Nuclear arms control also became more a medium for the superpowers to conduct "nuclear diplomacy" with each other than a true disarmament effort. That is, the state of arms control negotiations at any given time and the proposals (or lack of them) put forward by either side, became a central part of the superpowers' "managed competition" with each other. Each side planned and made its moves more as a way of *conducting* its competition with the other than as a way of *limiting* or partially *ending* the competition.

Another disadvantage is that the issue of nuclear arms control in the 1960s, 1970s, and 1980s absorbed much of the energy and attention of people seeking peace. Partly because of the complexity of nuclear arms control and partly because of the overwhelming, fascinating quality of the nuclear weapons and the images of nuclear war, nuclear arms control seized public attention almost completely. In many circles, arms control became almost synonymous with peace, and specific efforts to achieve the former came to replace more comprehensive efforts to achieve the latter. Consideration of other approaches and of other ways of conceiving the problem and its ultimate resolution was thereby hindered.

How successful can disarmament and true arms control be, insofar as one can judge by the record to date? Overall, it appears to be difficult for hostile and competing nations to restrain their arms races, however dangerous these races may be, except in cases where each nation sees a clear self-interest in doing so. The Non-Proliferation Treaty, for instance, is less an arms control agreement between the U.S. and the USSR than an agreement they jointly reached with much of the rest of the world that effectively preserves their nuclear supremacy. The ocean floor, outer space, and Latin America were domains where, for different reasons, each preferred not to compete anyway.

Disarmament and arms control are difficult partly because they must appeal to shared, mutual interests, while national governments by their nature tend to focus on unilateral advantage and disadvantage. This challenge might be surmountable if weapon types were few and clearly defined. But modern weapons are highly diverse in their capabilities. Hence comparisons of the arsenals of one nation with those of another inevitably end up being complicated and ambiguous. Those elements within either government that are inclined to suspect that a potential agreement puts their country at a disadvantage can usually find a way of interpreting the facts to that conclusion.

These problems existed even at the time of the Hague conference at the turn of the century; the technical problems posed by the weapons are far more complicated now than they were then. When one adds to this the fact that contemporary technology is evolving very rapidly, the task becomes much harder still. Many observers of strategic arms talks between the U.S. and USSR have concluded that it may have become impracticable for governments to decide on meaningful positions and conduct negotiations on nuclear arms; the technical environment simply changes too rapidly.

Thus on the whole we cannot expect too much from disarmament talks, at least under world circumstances like those of the 1980s. There is one possible exception to this generally pessimistic conclusion. That exception involves learning from experience—so far perhaps most strikingly the experience of crises and wars. In 1921 the public support for the Washington Conference naval formula was so great because people, having come through the suffering of a world war, were unusually determined that a similar war not occur again. The 1963 Limited Test Ban Treaty was made possible, most experts agree, by the Cuban Missile Crisis of 1962, which frightened governments and the public alike. Of course no one would recommend deliberate creation of crises simply to facilitate subsequent negotiations! However, as future crises are only too likely, it might be prudent to consider carefully what might best be done in their wake.

Perhaps the wisest overall conclusion is that it may be too much to ask that arms control and disarmament efforts alone bring about a true peace. They probably cannot be expected to work in an almost lawless and intensely competitive world political system that is short on devices for regulating and resolving conflict. This conclusion might be different in a changed world context in which an evolution in attitudes had created more effective means for coping with conflict. It seems plausible that then a well-thought-through arms control and disarmament program might be an essential ingredient in a more inclusive approach to creating a sustainable peace. We will return later to this possibility.

The Path of Removing Fundamental Causes of War

In addition to minimizing the incentives and means for war, one might also seek to maintain peace by minimizing or ameliorating the *underlying causes* of wars, insofar as this proves possible. Many years ago a U.S. political scientist, Kenneth Waltz, wrote a book now considered a classic: *Man, the State and War.* In it he organized all theories regarding the causes of war into three types. Some theories say that the basic causes of war lie in human nature; some theories locate the causes in the nature of the nation-state; and some locate the causes in the nature of the international system.

Theories attributing war to human nature generally posit that there is some form of aggressiveness, often thought to be innate, that erupts into war from time to time. The aggressiveness is seen as arising from different sources: territoriality, a drive for power, psychologically rooted hostilities, unconscious perceptions, or others. These theories and similar theories argue that the real source of war is not political as the nation-state and international system theories assert, but anthropological and/or psychological. Usually these theories are pessimistic about abolishing war (the aggressiveness is seen as innate) though they may hold out some hope for reducing its frequency or virulence. There is another variety of this type of theory that is far more optimistic; we will return to this in Chapters 4 and 5.

In the modern era there have been two main theories assigning the basic root of war to the nature of the nation-state. By selecting another kind of state, these theories say, wars could be ended. The "liberal" or democratic theory holds that democratic nations do not usually begin wars. The major wars of modern times have been launched by undemocratic nations against democratic ones (which then fought back) or against other undemocratic nations. This theory holds that basic political arrangements are essential, and economic affairs are unimportant in accounting for war. The Marxist theory claims the reverse. It holds that warfare is a product of the class struggle—when that struggle ends in the victory of the working classes, wars will also end, as they already have among socialist countries. Variations on these two main theories also arise, for instance the hypothesis that wars are caused directly or indirectly by "military-industrial complexes" within nations. All of these theories are, in principle, optimistic about removing the root causes of war, though they differ about what the roots, and hence the solutions, are.

The third kind of theory, also political, holds that the problem is not the nature of individual nation-states but the existence of many nation-states (of whatever kind) in a condition of near-anarchy together on the same planet. Nations coexisting in a state of anarchy must inevitably resort to violence from time to time just as individuals living in a state of anarchy inevitably would. The essential problem in world peace is that the forces of restraint and control in the global system are extremely weak, and many individual nations are very strong compared to those forces. Would one expect peace in a "society" of individuals in which some individuals, or gangs of them, were extremely powerful and the police almost nonexistent? Theories of this third kind are also optimistic, in principle, about removing the basic cause of war, as it should be possible to change the anarchic international system. The most commonly suggested alternative system is some form of world confederation or federalism, perhaps constructed from a revived or modified United Nations. However, advocates of these theories may be pessimistic in practice about the feasibility or likelihood of achieving this kind of change.

Objections can readily be found to all three types of theories. The objections range from lack of adequate evidence to existing counterevidence to the implausibility of suggested alternatives. It is not our purpose to summarize either the arguments pro and con or Waltz's analysis. Rather, in the remainder of this chapter we will come at the question of ameliorating fundamental causes of war by using a different approach, which cuts across Waltz's three levels and brings to light different factors than those usually raised by the kinds of theories just mentioned.

We focus upon what we will term *deeply felt social injustices*. These injustices involve collective psychology and may even have deep psychological or anthropological roots; they exist within many nations (in some nations they are all-important, in others almost nonexistent), and they are related to the nature of the international system. In many experts' opinions they are an especially important cause of war and one that will have to be dealt with if our world is ever to know lasting peace. Deeply felt social injustices seem to be of two main kinds: those that involve strong ethnic/religious hatreds and those that involve sharp economic disparities. Both the problems and, no doubt, the solutions are different in the two cases.

A remarkable proportion of the most terrible wars in history have been rooted in ethnic/religious hatreds: the Crusades, in which the flower of European youth was destroyed, one generation after another; the Thirty Years War, which utterly devastated Europe in the 1600s; and many of the great wars of earlier times. Perhaps an even more remarkable proportion of the wars of the second half of the twentieth century have also been rooted in ethnic/religious hatreds: three wars between India and Pakistan, three between Israel and Arab states, several in Africa, the Vietnam-Kampouchea war, and bloodiest of all, the Iran-Iraq War. In most of these examples, historical and recent, there have been other factors at work besides ethnic/religious hatreds. But study of these cases reveals that the other factors (rivalries, border disputes, and so on) may have provided triggers or immediate causes for the outbreak of war but do not explain the depth and duration of the fighting (in the Iran-Iraq and some African cases) or its repetition (in the India-Pakistan and Israeli-Arab cases). Ethnic/religious hatred is clearly central to explaining the bitterness and length of the fighting and the willingness to fight again and is probably an underlying cause of the fighting.

It probably is more useful to treat ethnic/religious hatred as a single problem than to try to distinguish how much is ethnic and how much is religious. Some African wars have been more ethnic than religious; the India-Pakistan wars have been more religious than ethnic; but even in these cases the other element has usually been present also. Hindus and Moslems, for instance, think of the difference between them in ways that a Westerner would regard as ethnic as well as religious. In the Israeli-Arab and Iran-Iraq cases the ethnic and religious elements are merged.

It may seem unusual to call these deep-seated ethnic/religious hatreds social injustices. Social injustice is often used as a code phrase for severe economic disparity, but that is only one form in which social injustice occurs or is perceived. Hatreds are felt as injustices by the societies that are the objects of hate. (If one individual hates another for the other's religious beliefs or color of skin, the recipient will feel an injustice is being done him; it is no different between societies.) The Arab attitude toward the Israelis, the Israeli attitude toward the Arabs, and the attitudes of Indians or Pakistanis involve deep feelings of actual and potential injustice. Ordinary Indian or Pakistani citizens, for instance, may consider themselves economically deprived compared to Westerners, but this does not lead nearly as easily to warlike feelings as does the sense of outrage they feel about the opposing country.

Of course, deep ethnic/religious hostilities lead to actions that create injustices of a more tangible kind, which in turn generate deeper hatreds. A classic example is Israel's treatment of the Palestinians, which—regardless of the intent—has created a situation for the Palestinians that they profoundly feel to be unjust. One result is that the generation of Palestinians that has grown up since feels hatred of Israel as their dominant political emotion and would be only too pleased to launch a war against Israel if war seemed practical.

The central role of ethnic/religious hatred as a cause of war demands more attention from peace specialists. There is a tendency to regard such hatred as a "brute fact," something about which nothing can be done and little even said. Also, religious matters are often seen as delicate subjects better left alone. But these attitudes are counter-productive in an age when even "small" wars may be extremely destructive and when more wars like some of those just named could trigger a global nuclear confrontation. Significant progress could be made in this area using new social and psychological concepts.

Social injustices in the more conventional sense of severe economic disparities have received much more attention in recent decades from peace specialists, although not nearly enough from Western society as a whole. Robert Heilbroner's book *An Inquiry Into the Human Prospect* was one of the first influential works to draw attention to the link between mass poverty in what we now call the Third World and the likelihood of future wars. Others have made this link often in the decade since, and the link has served to justify economic assistance from the developing world to underdeveloped nations.

The connection runs both ways between war and preparations for war on the one hand and the drastic economic difficulties of much of the Third World on the other. The resources sunk into armaments by many nations could yield immense benefits if applied to Third World development. Religious leaders, United Nations officials, and many specialists have tried repeatedly to draw attention to how much could be done to ease the world's sufferings if so much were not thrown into the maw of war. Vivid comparisons are offered, such as these from the Brandt Commission Report, *North-South:*

- The world military expenditure of only half a day would be enough to finance the entire malaria eradication program of the World Health Organization;
- For the price of just one jet fighter, 40,000 village pharmacies could be set up;
- For one-half of one percent of one year's world military expenditure, enough farm equipment could be purchased for all of the low-income nations that presently have insufficient food to approach food self-sufficiency in only ten years.

Many other comparisons like these are often drawn. As of this writing, however, expenditures on armaments are continuing to rise in almost all nations.

The connection between poverty and war is less direct and less immediately obvious in the other direction. It is difficult to find wars that were directly caused by poverty. National leaders have not—yet—declared that more national wealth is their war aim. Statistically there is no relationship between the degree of national poverty or wealth and the frequency of warfare. Poor nations fight even though they can't afford it, as Ethiopia, one of the world's poorest countries, has been demonstrating for many years. Rich nations fight even though they have no pressing economic needs to satisfy, as Britain demonstrated in the Falklands/Malvinas War.

Even so, it is hard to escape a conviction that the seeds of future wars already lie incubating in the grinding destitution of many peoples and their growing inability to meet even their simplest material needs. Wars may not be justified in those terms, but the frustration and rage that spring from these conditions and people's need to find solutions to at least some of their problems can help fuel wars especially where other tensions are already present. *North-South* puts it bluntly: "While hunger rules peace cannot prevail. He who wants to ban war must also ban mass poverty."[4]

Furthermore, coming decades could well see the emergence of new types of war in which deprivation played a more direct role. Under some conditions wars might be fought among comparatively poor nations explicitly for economic resources. Warlike acts could also be committed or threatened, in some circumstances, by poor nations against the rich nations in a fashion that the rich would call blackmail. For instance, a figure such as Colonel Khadaffi who came into possession of one or several nuclear weapons and was able to conceal them in U.S. cities might try to demand, say, ten billion dollars in material resources in return for not exploding them. Chemical or biological weapons might be usable in the same way. Actions of this sort would, of course, be explained to the world as a practical way of obtaining repayment for the "well-known exploitation of the Third World by the West." Not all Westerners realize that Third World anger is reaching a sufficient pitch that this justification would be accepted around much of the globe.

Strategists usually dismiss such hypothetical scenarios, perhaps correctly, on the ground that the "blackmailing" nation would be running the risk of terrible retribution. No national leader would want to incur such a danger and would be deterred. But even on the narrow logic of strategy, it seems hazardous to assume that the United States and its allies will always be able to deter or to defend against all potential threats from the Third World. Western interests are too extended, angry nations may become too numerous, and the potential weapons and tactics are too varied.

To those who desire peace the strategists' answer is more deeply unsatisfactory. It is not *peace* to propose a world of the near future in which the majority of humanity is impoverished and angry, while a few nations, almost unimaginably rich by the majority's standards, fortress themselves behind their retaliatory capacity.

The only answer, if peace is the goal, is for the nations of the rich North and the poor South to finds ways of working together to create a future that the majority can find satisfactory and moral. We do not suggest that this will be easy. But it is just as essential to a future world at peace as is an end to the nuclear arms race.

We do not wish to endorse the assumption, sometimes made, that this alternative is almost impossibly difficult. Few nations that find themselves making reasonable progress will jeopardize it by adopting long-term violent policies toward the West. Third World nations that have squandered what resources they had on their own large weapons arsenals will find that their moral claims are weak. And it is not necessary to assume that five billion or more people must live like Americans (which the planet may not be able to sustain ecologically anyway). A growing number of Moslem fundamentalists and others in the Third World reject the Western lifestyle as intolerably materialistic. Basic human needs, of course, must always be met, and on a global scale this by itself is a major challenge. But economic development in the usual Western sense is not the only path, and for some nations may not be the desirable path. What peace requires is that the nations and groupings of the Third World find the paths *they* chose open to them.

The two kinds of deeply felt social injustices—ethnic and religious hatred and severe economic disparities—represent underlying causes of war that may be especially important to cope with if our world is to have a future of peace. But one should not believe that even complete removal of these causes would by itself lead to that result. That belief assumes that war is not simply the result of deliberate decision by nation-states, but that war has to be "caused" by other factors. That assumption is questionable. Although some wars clearly seem to have roots, say, in evident ethnic/religious hatreds, others seem far removed from explanations about underlying causes, and seem most plausibly to be the result of calculated decisions by national governments. (Specialists sometimes call such wars *policy wars*.)

The U.S. invasion of Grenada in 1983 seems a clear example of a policy war, if it can be considered a war. Another, more painful example is the U.S. war in Vietnam. The United States is not an economically deprived country, and while some ethnic hatred among U.S. soldiers in Vietnam resulted from the war, it did not cause the war. Neither democratic nor Marxist explanations apply either, at least not in any very satisfactory way. The more democratic country chose to enter the conflict. Neither markets nor resources of any significance were at stake, and it was obvious very early that U.S. capitalism had more to lose than to gain from the escalating U.S. involvement. Grenada and Vietnam were both policy wars in which a decisionmaking elite made one or a series of calculated decisions based on concepts of power balances, cost/benefit ratios, and the containment or removal of regimes conceived to be hostile. An "explanation" of these U.S. wars, then, would consist primarily of analysis of the *intellectual* premises on which those calculations were made.

One should not assume, then, that a world in which there were no social injustices between nations would be a world automatically at peace. Quite possibly there could still be calculated wars of policy in such a world. However, one is safe in assuming that a future world that *did* continue to suffer from deeply felt social injustices would be a world *without* peace, at least without a peace that was reliable and lasting. Peace, as so many have pointed out, requires justice.

Summary

There are three traditional ways to prevent war: (1) reduce or eliminate the *incentives* to make war; (2) reduce the *means* available for waging war; and (3) reduce or eliminate the *fundamental causes* of war. Reducing incentives is approached largely through preventive diplomacy, which has undoubtedly prevented some wars in the past. The main problem with this method in a nuclear age is its limited scope. It may be a component of an overall approach to peace, but it cannot be relied upon alone. Reducing means is essentially arms control and disarmament. This method must be a component of any satisfactory overall strategy for sustainable peace, but it too cannot be depended on to do the job alone. Furthermore, the temptation to let arms control become the end goal instead of a step toward the goal of sustainable peace must be avoided. Reducing causes may be most important approach in the long term. Lasting peace will have to involve some satisfactory resolution of the modern world's perplexing human rights and development issues.

3

Alternative Paths
to Coping with Conflict

The four remaining paths to peace, discussed in this chapter and the next, are of a somewhat different sort. They all represent *alternatives* to the traditional ways of thinking about war, security, and peace. Because they are alternatives they have two characteristics in common that are not shared by the five approaches discussed so far.

In the first place, there are few if any historical instances where these approaches have been tried. Such historical support as can be found often involves analogies rather than actual cases. Discussion of these paths therefore tends toward the theoretical or toward the use of empirical evidence drawn from other fields. Nonviolent resistance is a partial exception, but the occasions when this method has been tried have usually been ones involving the domestic political order rather than the danger or actuality of war.

Second, by the mere fact of being alternatives to the established ways, these paths necessarily presuppose some sort of basic change in human affairs. At the least they presuppose, as in the case of the "moderate" version of alternative defense, an important change in technology. More typically they presuppose some significant changes in the political and social order, perhaps accompanied by psychological or cultural changes.

An approach to peace that is conditional on some major social/ political change may not be very plausible to a skeptical person. How, the skeptic asks, can we entrust our peace and security to untried, hypothetical, and perhaps hopelessly idealistic schemes?

To this question, advocates of the alternative paths make several responses. It may be pointed out, for example, that profound social changes have happened before in history—the abolition of slavery, say, or the shift from feudalism to capitalism. There is no reason to assume that we have seen the last of such changes. A different response to international conflict could be a key characteristic of the next of these shifts.

Also, it may be argued that a new approach is clearly demanded by the overwhelming danger that war now poses. War, however evil it may have been, might be tolerated when the destruction it wrought was limited. But the threat of nuclear war now jeopardizes the whole of civilization and possibly even the survival of the human species. This unprecedented danger necessitates a new way of dealing with conflict.

Finally, the argument may be put forth that humanity is now ready for a new approach that would not have been accepted earlier. Such an argument is supported by indications of significant value and attitude shifts over the last few decades.

As none of these alternative paths have been tried on a significant scale, how one weighs these various arguments will depend very much on such intangible factors as intuitive judgment about the validity of the arguments and analogies and deeply held preferences and values.

This chapter presents a path for coping with *existing* conflict and one for coping with *imminent* conflict. (See again Table 1.) The paths involve, respectively, alternative defense and nonviolent resistance. These two approaches are very similar in some respects. However, the latter by definition involves no violence; the former has a different relationship to violence. Both of these paths contain an element of deterrence, although of a very different sort than nuclear deterrence.

The Path of Alternative Defense

Alternative defense is a term that has become commonly used in the 1980s. It is an umbrella label for a somewhat loose grouping of ideas that have in common two basic premises:

- That an alternative must be found to warfare as it is now conceived by the technically advanced powers because that warfare would be very destructive;

- That the concept of defense, involving at least a threat of violence, is legitimate.

To date nearly all theorists of alternative defense are either Europeans (to some extent East as well as West Europeans) or, to a lesser degree, Americans. And most of the theorizing presupposes Europe or some part of it as the locale where alternative defense is to be applied. This is not accidental. Europe is one of the most densely militarized regions on Earth (along with some parts of the Middle East) and is the region where the most advanced military technology is deployed. The destruction that technology would wreak, were it used, is staggering to contemplate.

As early as the mid-1950s, when the United States first began deploying "tactical" or "theater" nuclear weapons in Europe, the destruction potential of those weapons was already known to be enormous. A military exercise of that period postulated several million deaths among West German civilians alone as an unavoidable by-product of using the few hundred weapons deployed at that time. Since then, both the United States and the Soviet Union have installed thousands of additional theater nuclear weapons of all kinds in Europe (and in the western parts of the USSR for use against targets in Europe). Although the great majority of these are intended for use against military targets, Europe is so densely populated that most military targets are not far from towns and cities. The collateral damage (as it is termed in military jargon) would be tremendous. In addition, an ample number of weapons have been reserved for deliberate targeting of population centers.

By the late 1970s it was becoming evident to specialists that the collateral deaths and destruction that would be caused by *conventional* warfare in Europe was growing rapidly as well. Advancing conventional weapons technology was producing more lethal weapons. Some of the conventional weapons to be deployed in Europe in great numbers in the 1990s begin to approximate small nuclear weapons in their destructive power.

The extent of the destruction would be much more widespread than may be apparent to one imagining a battle confined to a "front" between East and West. For a long time the Warsaw Pact has planned, and increasingly the North Atlantic Treaty Organization (NATO) is also planning, deep strikes far into the other side's territory by missiles, aircraft, and airborne troops. This defense via a tactical offense would spread the effects of the fighting over most of Europe.

Thus by the mid-1980s it had been generally accepted among military and arms control specialists of all political persuasions that any future all-out conventional war in Europe between the Warsaw Pact and NATO could cause a level of death and destruction not much less than what might be caused by a nuclear war. (This assumption does not consider the possible use of chemical and maybe even biological weapons, which would increase the carnage tremendously. Soviet military doctrine, as evidenced by preparations and deployments, seems to envisage any sizable European war as involving the use of chemical weapons.)

The conclusion drawn by some peace theorists is that defense in the usual military sense of the term, especially defense by offensive tactics, is becoming more and more difficult to justify morally (and politically, especially in democracies). Military technology is "progressing" to the point where conventional offensive warfare between technically advanced nations, especially in a geographically limited area, is not a permissible defense option. Thus there is a need to find some sort of alternative defense.

Alternative defense research has generally attempted to define a form of defense that would (1) greatly *reduce the casualties* in the event of war and (2) present a genuinely *stronger posture* from which to successfully defend at least one's own national territory. (A strong defense posture would represent a strong deterrent.)

The first of these goals is identical to one of the goals of arms control. Recognizing that however much we may try to prevent it, war could occur, alternative defense—like arms control—seeks to reduce the costs of war as far as possible. (In this respect, both approaches create a certain paradox. If one believes that the preservation of peace is best assured when war is made intolerably costly and horrible, then reducing the costs of war may seem to be detrimental.)

The second goal of alternative defense is to rescue the idea of defense from the disrepute into which it has fallen. In the last few decades, defense has often been used as a euphemism for war. (The United States renamed its War Department the Department of Defense in 1947.) The reigning defense doctrine—nuclear deterrence—is really a doctrine of preventing war by extreme threat of *offensive* action. Nations all over the world now routinely describe their military actions as being defensive in intention, even when the actions are taken at a great distance (for example, the U.S. war in Vietnam). Alternative defense theorists hope to resurrect the older idea that it is entirely moral to defend oneself, especially when doing so does not involve threatening or attacking others.

Alternative defense theory, therefore, really *is* theory about defense. Broadly speaking, two forms can be identified, that might be called its "moderate" and "extreme" versions. The moderate form retains the concept of a strong military organization, but with doctrine, deployment, and capabilities exclusively defensive. The extreme form of alternative defense does away with a powerful organized military and relies instead upon an armed citizenry, a popular militia, or at most some form of paramilitary units. What unites these two forms of the theory is that both accept the validity of nationally organized violent action in self-defense, but reject any form of offensive action or offensive threat. They assert that a strictly defensive posture is the most moral and the strongest national posture possible.

Why it is the most moral may be obvious: Such a posture threatens no one and cannot lead to war unless war is begun by someone else. The right to self-defense is accepted as moral in most religious and ethical traditions, except those committed to nonviolence. Advocates of alternative defense usually regard themselves as committed proponents of peace, pointing out that if their concept were accepted by every nation, war would be rendered impossible. Purely defensive military postures, adopted even by neighbors harboring hostile feelings toward each other, will not result in war. (It is primarily for this reason that the concept of alternative defense is included here as a path to peace even though the concept is a military one.)

It may be less obvious why such a posture should be the strongest one possible. Several reasons for this are advanced by the advocates of this path. One is that a purely defensive posture is the only one that virtually all of a nation's citizens will support indefinitely. A posture containing any kind of offensive component—even if based, like nuclear deterrence, on the intention to prevent war—is in danger of losing consensus support sooner or later. (Indeed, nuclear deterrence did lose some of its support among the U.S. public in the 1980s.) But nearly everyone will support defense of their own homeland. This policy, therefore, is uniquely suited to achieving political unity in the face of a severe threat.

There are also several practical reasons why an alternative defense posture should be the strongest one. A country defending itself against a neighboring aggressor is fighting on its home ground. The defenders are bound to know the territory better than the invaders. They will also be more highly motivated because they are fighting to protect their own homes. History offers many examples of a country that is fighting for its own survival outlasting an invading army whose motivation is less profound and cannot be sustained as long. Finally, there is a gradient by which power falls off with distance: The further that national power must be projected away from its home territory (with bases, supply sources, and so on), the less power can be delivered. Naturally this works in favor of the defender and against the attacker.

There is a limitation to these arguments in that they presuppose that the warring nations are roughly equal in power. Often that is not the case. For instance, the United States was able to capture the island of Okinawa during World War II—even though Okinawa was only about fifteen hundred miles from the Japanese homeland and was ten thousand miles from the United States—because by that point in the war the U.S. was vastly stronger than Japan. Many other such examples could be cited. This problem of great disparities in power is the principal reason that acceptance for an alternative defense approach has been growing so slowly. Rough equality of power seems to be a precondition for practical alternative defense. This problem is also the principal reason for the divergence between the two forms of alternative defense policy.

Advocates of the extreme form of alternate defense visualize citizens defending themselves and their nation in highly decentralized fashion. Slightly different variants of this image emphasize guerrilla warfare or some kind of semiorganized citizens' army or militia. The result in the event of an invasion would be roughly the same. Fighters would be almost indistinguishable from ordinary citizens, and practically every citizen would be a potential fighter. Organization would exist at a local and perhaps regional level, but there would be little or none at the national level. The invading army would be unable to find any headquarters or hard core of the resistance to defeat; the resistance would be everywhere and nowhere. Supporters of this image cite, for instance, the tremendous difficulty, and ultimate failure, that even the powerful U.S. forces experienced in locating and defeating the Viet Cong in Vietnam in the 1960s and early 1970s.

Critics of this image point out that the Viet Cong had outside assistance and that the United States was constrained in various ways that a more ruthless attacker would not be. They argue that a more accurate comparison would be Afghanistan in the 1980s, which was a situation exactly like that advocated by the extreme form of alternative defense theory. A tenacious, highly decentralized resistance saw itself as defending its own homeland against a hated outside invader. Furthermore, the invading nation deployed many fewer troops than the resistance had. All the themes should apply— the greater motivation and staying power of the resistance, knowing one's territory, and not having to fight at a distance. Yet in fact, as of this writing the Afghan resistance is gradually but steadily losing to the invading forces, who do not restrain themselves from demolishing towns and villages, carpet-bombing many populated areas, and in other ways employing the most ruthless measures. The Afghans are gradually losing, in fact, despite receipt of substantial military aid from China, Arab countries, and the U.S. However, if this aid is increased the outcome may change, and it should be pointed out that the Afghan resistance was not prepared for the war and is severely divided internally.

Advocates of the moderate form of alternative defense conclude from cases like Afghanistan that a militarily powerful, technologically advanced, and sufficiently ruthless invader will probably defeat a population-based decentralized defense if prepared to take the time and pay a significant price to do so. But a strictly defensive strategy *can* succeed, these advocates say, if it is organized along regular military lines by a nation or alliance roughly equal in power to the potential attacker.

The case that primarily interests these theorists is Western Europe—or rather, as U.S. assistance is usually presupposed, NATO. Proponents of this form of alternative defense argue that NATO should replace its present strategy with a quite different one. Since the mid-1950s NATO has insisted that it must reserve the right of "first use" of nuclear weapons because it could not mount sufficient conventional power to match the Soviet conventional threat. In the 1980s NATO adopted the deep-strike policy of the Warsaw Pact.

An alternative strategy is made possible by emerging technologies that would enable a nonnuclear defense to be successful. (These technologies include vastly improved homing systems for conventional warheads and increased armor penetration.) Although past technological advance has most often improved offensive rather than defensive weapons the new technologies may favor defense over offense. The technical and military details are outside the scope of this book and in any case are subjects of dispute. There is some question, for instance, whether some of the new conventional technologies that are powerful enough to comprise effective defense might not wreak collateral damage comparable to that which alternative defense strategy is designed to avoid.

The advocates argue that a military/technical posture can be designed that would be considerably more decentralized than NATO currently is and that would employ some—not all—of the emerging technologies. This posture, it is argued, could command greater and more lasting political support within NATO countries than the nuclear first-use doctrine can. It would serve as an effective deterrent, helping to ensure that there is no war. If through accident or miscalculation a war did somehow break out, a NATO policy of no-first-use of nuclear weapons should provide time for high-level negotiations to halt the war.

Critics of this viewpoint who advocate the more extreme form of alternative defense (as well as other critics who favor disarmament, nonviolence, or other approaches) sometimes say that this proposed redesign of NATO strategy is really just a variation on the status quo. It is, they argue, simply a different military strategy aimed at solving a military problem. (They compare it with the Maginot Line, which also represented a strictly defensive approach and employed the most advanced technology of its day.) They point out that without more fundamental change, NATO strategy will need to be remodified if technology begins to favor offense again and thus that the solution is temporary.

Other critics contend that the concept of a defensive deterrent for NATO is philosophically too much like the Strategic Defense Initiative conception of the Reagan administration and might in effect promote such concepts. Indeed, the rise in interest in a defensive strategy for NATO roughly coincides with the arrival of SDI and may reflect some deeper shift toward a more defensive overall way of thinking. Some experts also foresee the possibility of a more defensive NATO posture being linked technically and militarily to a "Star Wars" missile defense for Europe. For reasons like these, the more moderate form of alternative defense may not seem, to some readers, to really be a path to peace. To these readers, the more extreme version of alternative defense may still be of interest in two possible applications.

First, this theory may be applied to *some* situations even if it is not applicable to all. That it is failing for the Afghans does not mean that it always must fail. It may only mean that the strategy would work best for a country with larger population and territory. It has been pointed out, for instance, that in many ways the ideal country for this form of alternative defense is the United States. The U.S. can be *destroyed* (by nuclear weapons) but it probably cannot be *conquered*. It has no comparably powerful neighbors, and deploying enough troops for occupation would be extraordinarily difficult for any distant nation even if the Americans refrained from fighting until the invader was actually on their soil. (This observation probably applies also to the USSR.) Furthermore, U.S. popular culture with its Wild West tradition, emphasis on individual initiative, and a hundred million handguns currently in private hands, probably makes the United States the most favorable test case for arguing a policy of armed civilian resistance.

Against this line of reasoning it should be asked whether recommending such a strategy, even for the United States, should properly be regarded as a path to peace. As an alternative to a policy of nuclear deterrence the proposition is at least debatable, but put forth as a peace strategy it seems questionable. Effective alternative defense of this form would require sizable preparations in advance among the entire civilian population. Arguably, these preparations could well create (and the actual armed resistance almost certainly would create) a widespread state of mind and a type of social order that would be more violent and militarized than today's situation.

The second, and more important, potential application of alternative defense concepts is to incorporate them in a larger plan. For example, alternative defense might conceivably be linked to a version of disarmament that included the verified abolition of certain entire categories of weapons—namely those weapons that could defeat an alternative defense strategy. As we have observed earlier, the notion of nine "pure" approaches to peace is an artificial device useful for clarifying our thinking. No doubt any realistic solution would employ elements of a number of approaches.

The Path of Nonviolent Action

A seventh path sometimes discussed in connection with peace is that of nonviolent action. Nonviolent action is not passive resistance; indeed it is not passive at all. It is an active, assertive approach to wielding political, economic, and moral/psychological power and depends heavily on taking initiatives, often ambitious ones. Nonviolent action also is not "pacifism" if pacifism is interpreted to mean the rejection of all force or coercion; many nonviolent actions are coercive (for example, going on strike or blockading roads with human bodies).

It may seem odd to count this path as an alternative one because it is quite old. There have been countless instances of nonviolent action throughout history, many quite successful. Even so, it is best regarded as an "alternative path" for two reasons.

One reason is that people tend to forget these historical attempts (or to recall the outcome without identifying the preceding process as an example of nonviolent action). Most people think immediately of only one historical set of nonviolent actions, namely that occurring during the life of Gandhi. (Most Americans can recall Martin Luther King Jr. as well.) By contrast, any person with at least a high school education can easily remember the names of a dozen wars. Violence seems to be the regular and accepted approach, nonviolence the exceptional one.

The other reason that nonviolence must be regarded as an alternative path to peace is that it has only partially and occasionally been presented as an approach to solving the problem of *war*. Rather, it has usually been presented as an intrinsically peaceful approach to accomplishing political change. Gandhi sought Indian independence from British rule; Martin Luther King sought full equality for U.S. blacks. Neither man offered nonviolent action as the centerpiece of a solution to the problem of war, nor have most other leaders. But because this approach appears to offer the prospect of great political change without war and without violence, it must be— and increasingly is being—considered by those searching for ways to attain and preserve peace.

The main reason nonviolence has seemed somewhat tangential to the problem of war is that, generally speaking, nonviolent action can be taken only when the contending parties are both occupying the same territory. The British were occupying India, a fact that seemingly added to British power but that also made the British accessible and vulnerable to Indian nonviolent actions. Whites and blacks were living together in U.S. cities, which made segregationist whites accessible and vulnerable to nonviolent civil rights actions. This characteristic of the mingling of the contending groups applies to the great majority of known cases of nonviolent action.

Thus nonviolent action can usually be advanced as a possibility only after one side has taken possession of part or all of the other side's territory. Advocates of nonviolence normally *begin* their scenario of events with a successful invasion of one nation by another. That is to say, the invading army has occupied all the territory it seeks to occupy, either because the defending army has been defeated or because the invaded country, following the policy of nonviolence, has not tried to defend itself by military means. The time when penetration is complete is the time when nonviolent action can begin.

Depending on the details of the situation, many possibilities may arise. In 1968, when the Soviet Union invaded Czechoslovakia, a portion of the Czech population improvised a variety of nonviolent actions. The Czech media defied the Soviet order to make public announcements that Czech leaders had invited the Soviet action. The National Assembly met, denounced the invasion, and demanded withdrawal of the troops. There were large nonviolent demonstrations and brief general strikes by workers. The Czech police aided the resisters rather than the Soviets. The main result of these and many other actions was to deny the Soviets, for about eight months, one of their important goals: creation of a "Czech" puppet government to which the people would acquiesce and that would declare the Soviet action legitimate. But intense and sustained Soviet pressure did achieve this goal in the end; there was probably never any expectation that the Soviets could really be induced to withdraw. Advocates of nonviolent action argue, however, that important strategic mistakes were made by the resistance and that in any case the Czech people and leadership had not planned for their nonviolent action to be sustained indefinitely.

The fact that the argument for nonviolent action begins with an actual invasion is significant in several ways. To begin with, it means that this path resembles, in some ways, the more extreme version of alternative defense. Both theories start from the premise that an enemy army has successfully invaded. Both theories also postulate the involvement of almost the whole population in the resistance (rather than an organized and disciplined minority called "the military"). Both theories claim that a potential enemy will be deterred by the prospect of having to take on the resistance of an entire people, and hence there will be no war in the first place. Where these approaches differ drastically is on the *means* to be employed: decentralized but widespread, sustained violence versus systematic nonviolent action.

There is one significant strength and two important weaknesses that apply equally to both nonviolent action and the extreme form of alternative defense. The strength is a moral one. Defense of one's homeland against an external invader is the most respected justification for struggle; no reason for any kind of action outside one's own borders commands as much acceptance. Resistance on one's own territory not only ensures the greatest degree of political unity at home but it also guarantees the maximum degree of respect for the struggle on the part of other countries. This respect has often been translated into material support.

But with this strength goes a weakness that applies to the time before the enemy's attack comes—the time when the violent or nonviolent civilian resistance is being prepared and organized. The weakness is that people do not like being obliged to consider how they will resist *after* the enemy is already among them. The view more likely to be widely held (the "commonsense" point of view) is that the time and place to stop the enemy is *before* it has invaded. If an enemy can be halted at, or preferably far from, the border, then the homeland will be spared great agony, the war will have been won, and peace will be restored. Both nonviolent action and the extreme form of alternative defense hold out the prospect of tremendous suffering to the very people who will have to carry out the actions involved. That the large number of civilians who must resist, nonviolently or violently, must suffer is a major precondition for the success of either of these paths. While it is possible to make sacrifice and suffering morally appealing for a time, the prospect that they may continue indefinitely has much less appeal.

There is a second weakness in these two approaches. They are primarily concerned with invasion by land armies. This restriction is not an intellectual accident: *Only* this form of attack can be met by armed civilian resistance or nonviolent civilian action. In the second half of the twentieth century, such a land attack is certainly not the only important kind of aggression to anticipate. How is a nation using alternate methods of defense to cope with attacks from the sea by cruise or ballistic missiles, attacks from the air, or attacks by long-range missiles launched from the enemy nation?

Occasionally this query prompts the response that the enemy, to really win, must actually invade with its armies, even if there is a preliminary "softening up" bombardment from a distance. But this may not be true, depending on what the aggressor's political objectives are. The aggressor nation may not seek political control of the victim nation, but may only seek to weaken it gravely. A ruthless, technologically advanced aggressor nation may wish to make itself the undisputed dominant power in its region and thus be content to destroy or severely damage from a distance the military and economic power of all rivals. The paths of nonviolent or violent action by a population would hardly be able to counteract this danger. It is certainly conceivable that a sufficiently powerful and ruthless country could seek to dominate the world in this fashion.

The possibility of a nation run amuck, seeking to dominate the entire world through intimidation, may seem improbable and bizarre. That impression may result mainly from its novelty. A devastating "stand-off" attack has only become technologically possible very recently. It is perfectly feasible now, and in the (probably continuing) absence of any effective defense against a massive missile or air attack, it will continue to be feasible. (In the absence of verifiable disarmament of such weapons of attack, this possibility is perhaps the most powerful argument for the approach of deterrence.) Few doubt that a dictator as ruthless as Hitler might have employed such an approach if he believed it would succeed. More recently, Idi Amin, Khadaffi, and Khomeini have reminded us that national leaders roughly comparable to Hitler in their aggressiveness may not be too uncommon.

This weakness creates a great difficulty for any claim that either nonviolent action or alternative defense can represent a general solution to the problem of war. However, neither can any one of the traditional paths, including deterrence, provide a general solution. If either the path of nonviolent action or that of alternative defense were to be *combined* with a general disarmament of those weapons suitable for stand-off attack, then some of the objections to the alternative approaches would be removed.

There are two powerful arguments for developing and implementing the path of nonviolent action. The first is that, unlike the more extreme form of alternative defense, nonviolent action (despite its long history) is not very well understood. It may well be rendered stronger through being better known.

The inadequate understanding of nonviolent action exists for a number of reasons. First of all, the records are sparse. Many of the attempts at nonviolent action have not been preserved in historical records, or have been recorded so sketchily that it is impossible to discern the circumstances that made for success or failure. (Violence, by contrast, is typically well recorded.) Of the known efforts, most were single actions taken in isolation or a scattering of actions taken with little or no coherence among them. Since there is an enormous menu of nonviolent actions possible, single or scattered actions may not tell us much; in many cases the wrong actions for the circumstances may have been taken. Few leaders seem to have understood how various actions might be *integrated* into a systematic campaign, *sequenced* over time for cumulative effect. Most nonviolent actions have been improvised by groups that knew little of the history of nonviolence and hence could not draw confidence from many important successes. Finally, much is not yet understood about how and why nonviolent action works. What is clear is that it succeeds primarily by the moral effect of the action—on observing audiences, on the nonviolent actors themselves, and perhaps most importantly on those against whom the action is taken. But the psychological and other processes involved are poorly understood.

Of the nine paths, nonviolence is one, along with the ninth, about which the least is known. Violent methods have been studied to an incomparably greater degree and refined with tremendous sophistication. Faced with such ignorance about an approach that has scored notable successes even in primitive applications, one can only conclude that this path deserves much greater development.

The second argument leading to the same conclusion is that coping with an invader through nonviolent action has virtually never been attempted by a *prepared* population. The significant known cases of a people resisting an invader by nonviolent means are all instances in which a nation that had not contemplated nonviolent resistance beforehand was invaded—whereupon some groups conceived and tried various relatively spontaneous nonviolent actions. Presumably a nation that had adequately prepared itself would be in an enormously stronger position.

Advocates of nonviolent action make the point that the issue of preparation makes any simple comparison between the effectiveness of violent and nonviolent approaches problematic. Persons making such comparisons (often as a way to disparage the effectiveness of nonviolence) tend to forget that the successes of the military methods they praise were the result of thorough, systematic, and expensive advance preparation. Improvised military defenses have rarely succeeded in defeating the opponent. Why, then, should it be surprising that improvised nonviolent actions *also* have rarely succeeded in defeating the opponent? The strongest case for the path of nonviolent action, then, must be a case for a prepared resistance campaign, comparable in some respects to a prepared military campaign and applicable to a situation where invasion is the danger.

Some current theorists have coined the phrase "civilian-based defense" as a label for a prepared nonviolent resistance campaign. This should not be confused with the alternative-defense option of preparing an *armed* civilian resistance. There are historical examples of the failure of efforts to combine armed resistance and nonviolent resistance. In general it appears that violent and nonviolent methods each tend to undercut the effectiveness of the other and hence cannot be successfully mixed, at least not in the same geographical area.

A nation choosing a civilian-based defense would have to develop a plan for integrated, sequenced nonviolent actions and educate virtually the entire population in the meaning, purposes, and execution of this plan. Naturally the plan must be flexible enough to adapt to the invader's counteractions. The goal of this type of defense is deterrence; peace would be preserved if the potential enemy decides that the price of occupying the target country and coping with the continual resistance is too high.

If, however, deterrence fails and the aggressor does invade, there would still be no war in the ordinary sense; there would be no violence perpetrated by the resisting population. (Violence committed by the occupying forces is to be expected.) The populace would make the occupation as difficult, troublesome, and costly to the invader as possible, short of harming the troops physically. The menu of possible actions is a very long one. A short sample of the possibilities includes

- Acts of sabotage against the invaded country's transportation systems, timed and located to give maximum trouble to the occupying forces;
- Acts of sabotage against the print and television media, including selective refusals to reprint or broadcast the invader's messages;
- Acts of sabotage against the occupier-controlled portion of the country's information and computer systems, including extensive computer "hacking";
- Selective but repeated and massive strikes by workers of all levels, possibly including selective use of the general strike;
- Systematic efforts to explain to the occupying troops, individual by individual, that the "justification" for the invasion is false

propaganda, that there is no threat to their own nation and that their presence is deeply resented. (It is impossible for the invader to separate his troops from the "host" population if there is not active cooperation by some domestic element such as a puppet government.) Hostility toward the *occupation* can be combined with seductive fraternization with the *occupiers* to render the enemy's troops unreliable and eventually rebellious;

- Selective destruction and sabotage of particular national resources and commodities that the invader is exploiting;
- Persistent, systematic use of protest marches, demonstrations, and every feasible device of public protest.

Many variations on and combinations of these ideas are possible, and this list is by no means exhaustive. In the end, the path of nonviolent action is based on the principle that a population that is persistently determined not to be conquered cannot be. There are always further means of resistance. A civilian-based defense of this kind cannot physically defeat the invader's army and force it out of the country but can possibly make the cost of the occupation so high that the aggressor will give up. (Providing the invader with a face-saving way to withdraw is an important part of the nonviolent approach.)

Several potential problems with this approach (other than its irrelevance to stand-off bombardment) should be mentioned briefly. First of all, is this really a path to peace? A civilian population that is resisting in this fashion will certainly not be at peace in the sense of absence of conflict. On the contrary, a state of affairs will exist that in many social and psychological respects resembles war. The occupied populace will have to devote a considerable fraction of whatever time, energy, and material resources it can still control to the resistance. The situation will be abnormal, very tense, and for those seriously involved in resistive acts, extremely dangerous.

A related problem is the threat of genocide. A population determined to resist cannot be conquered but can be exterminated, or enough people can be killed to make the rest submit. The answer given to this challenge by advocates of nonviolent action is that a large fraction of the invader's troops will not be willing to carry out a policy of deliberate genocide. However, small fractions may be. Events transpiring during the Soviet invasion of Afghanistan; in Lebanon at various times; on other occasions in the Middle East, Southeast Asia, and Africa in recent decades; and most of all in Hitler's Europe surely raise the possibility that genocide is possible.

Finally, systematic civilian nonviolence depends crucially on relatively free communications among the groups and leaders of the resisting population. Actions that cannot be planned, coordinated, and communicated to those who will act can scarcely be carried out. Also, nonviolent actions must receive public attention to be effective; a national campaign of nonviolent actions cannot achieve its goals if every action is effectively concealed. Such a campaign depends upon political momentum generated by a populace that is aware that many people are participating and that many nonviolent actions are occurring.

For these reasons, critics often argue that the path of systematic nonviolent action is one that is likely to work only against a comparatively civilized opponent who places definite limits on the amount of repression imposed and allows the conquered population a significant degree of freedom. The validity of this criticism, like so much about the path of nonviolent action, remains to be discovered.

4

Alternative Paths
to Preventing Conflict

We turn now to two approaches to preventing the emergence of conflict or resolving conflict before it threatens to lead toward war. The first of these approaches involves a family of ideas that collectively can be called conflict resolution systems. The second approach is different in kind from any previously examined—it involves a transformation of attitudes or consciousness. These two paths can potentially be combined with the traditional paths discussed in Chapter 2—preventive diplomacy, disarmament/arms control, and advancing social justice—but are alternative in that they differ from the traditional approaches and contain new and emerging elements.

The Path of Alternative Conflict Resolution

Alternative thinking about the problem of maintaining and preserving peace among nations begins with the observation that traditional approaches have not proved very successful and that something different is needed. As pointed out in previous chapters, the need to find effective paths to peace is critical and urgent. Recognition of the inadequacy of past attempts to arrive at sustainable peace prompts a serious search for alternatives.

Both traditional and alternative approaches to the problem employ as their starting point the premise that nations need specifiable, workable methods for resolving conflicts. After all, if significant conflicts did not arise, the whole problem of peace and war would not come up in the first place and peace, like gravity, would be part of the natural order. Effort is required to maintain peace because conflicts are continually arising.

One may imagine a spectrum of the intensity or seriousness of conflict, beginning at the mildest possible point where a disagreement has barely emerged, ranging through gradually deepening and intensifying dispute, and ending finally at the eruption of violence. The goal of conflict resolution is to intervene in this spectrum of potential escalation at the lowest possible point and to resolve the dispute before it escalates further.

Perhaps the most significant issue on which the traditional and alternative approaches to conflict resolution differ involves the focus on the nation-state as the principal actor in the system. The traditional paths adopt this focus almost exclusively. Disarmament/ arms control, for example, is a type of action to be undertaken by nations. Other forces (such as world opinion) may impinge upon the nation and affect its decisions, but the nation-state remains the principal actor. The alternative approaches to conflict resolution acknowledge that nations will almost certainly remain significant actors in the world scene for some time to come but emphasize that significant roles could be played by other actors both at a more global level and at a lower level.

Many proponents of alternative conflict resolution argue that the traditional systems are seriously handicapped by their exclusive concentration on the nation-state and its sovereignty. International law, for example, is supposed to be a conflict resolution system. International law provides a set of mechanisms, culminating in judgment by the International Court of Justice, by which nations can resolve their disputes through an orderly process. In theory, such a system ought to be able to resolve conflicts between nations without any threat of—or resort to—violence. In practice the system's effectiveness is limited by the unwillingness of nations to relinquish sovereignty and accept judgments contrary to their immediate interests.

The original intention behind the Security Council mechanism within the United Nations was that it too would serve as a key component in a conflict resolution system. The intent was that any nation that failed to use the mechanisms of orderly diplomacy and international law to resolve some dispute and instead pressed claims to the point of threatening war would become the subject of Security

Council attention. The council, representing the world's great powers, would be able to threaten severe sanctions (explicitly including military action, according to the UN Charter) if that nation continued to endanger the peace. The point of this threat would be deterrence. A potential aggressor nation, faced by the combined strength of the world's great powers, presumably would not dare to carry out its threat of violence. In effect the potential aggressor would be compelled to avoid the path of violence and to turn to legitimated negotiating processes (or perhaps drop its claims).

International law and the UN Security Council are traditional mechanisms, and it is generally agreed that neither has even remotely succeeded in achieving their intended purposes. In neither case have the powerful nations been willing to limit their sovereignty to the degree that would be necessary for supranational mechanisms to function effectively. International law is, in fact, rarely employed by nations with disputes serious enough that they might become causes for war. The law mechanism does not include any strong incentive for nations to use it nor any device to force them to do so. The Security Council, which in principle could provide a strong incentive, has been rendered unable to do so by the continuing global conflict between two of its veto-wielding permanent members, the United States and the Soviet Union. At no time has the council achieved the unanimity necessary to threaten military sanctions against a nation contemplating war.

The conflict resolution system represented by international law fails, then, because policy-makers potentially at conflict perceive *much stronger incentives to win on the issue by any effective means* (including war or the threat of war) *than to employ a peace-maintaining means* (the law system) through which they might or might not win. Essentially the same observation applies to the Security Council. The policy-makers of the United States and the Soviet Union have stronger incentives to permit a local conflict (in the outcome of which one or both superpowers often have an interest) to escalate toward violence than to employ the threat of jointly supported Security Council military action to preserve the local peace.

It has been so long, in fact, since either international law or the threat of direct Security Council military sanctions has been used to head off an escalating conflict that to most policy-makers in most countries neither seems a real option. The mere suggestion to use these mechanisms in this way seems antiquated or quixotic.

Observing this, theorists of alternative conflict resolution systems advance a variety of proposals for improved and/or new mechanisms. Any particular mechanism may represent only a part of a full system, but it is usually argued that the addition and proper integration of more and more conflict resolution mechanisms can effectively add up to an increasingly effective, eventually complete, conflict resolution system.

The least radical of such proposals suggests more widespread and systematic use of mediation and related techniques. As noted in Chapter 2, mediation has been increasingly used by nations in recent decades; it could be used much more extensively still. This is an area where some progress is being made. As recently as a generation ago, policy-makers of a nation with a serious dispute typically saw any suggestion of mediation by a third party as a hostile step. Now they rarely do (although they may not accept the suggestion). Progress is also being made in developing the techniques of mediation; the "state of the art" has advanced considerably in the last couple of decades. Theorists argue that both the growing acceptability and the growing capabilities of mediation should justify much more frequent use of this conflict resolution technique.

Without detracting from the merits of international law, it may be observed that mediation has at least one significant advantage over law as a conflict resolution mechanism: Mediation leaves more discretion in the hands of the disputing parties, and hence is less likely to be perceived as a challenge to sovereignty. In an international law system, the contending nations prepare their arguments, and then the issue passes out of their hands as it works its way through the court system. By contrast, a mediator attempts to find and enlarge areas of agreement between the contending parties; to find points of dispute that can be postponed, reinterpreted, or otherwise rendered less immediately contentious; and to keep the negotiation going in a way that promises both sides the prospect of a reasonably satisfactory outcome. Each party is constantly in contact with the mediator—and perhaps with each other. Each is constantly able to press its views or perhaps modify them. Each side retains substantial control over the process, even to the point of being able to withdraw.

This retention of sovereignty and initiative, which might at first blush seem to make mediation more likely than law systems to perpetuate the conflict, in fact makes mediation more attractive to the disputing parties. Mediation tends to create confidence that each party can retain enough control to ensure that it will not be forced to accept a disadvantageous outcome. Arguably, then, mediation may be a more effective conflict resolution device than law in many cases.

A more radical mechanism that might be effectively used under some circumstances is a kind of nonviolent action. In addition to the nonviolent defense discussed previously, under certain conditions there can be offensive nonviolence as well, sometimes called *peaceful invasion*. Although offensive in intent, this technique represents an alternative to violence or war; although it temporarily escalates the conflict, it is intended to lead to the resolution of the conflict while preserving peace. The possibilities and limits of the peaceful invasion process can be illustrated by two cases, one of success and one of failure.

The success occurred in northwestern Africa in 1975. A territory called Spanish Sahara, bordering the kingdom of Morocco on the south, had long been under the colonial control of Spain. Spain suddenly announced that it had decided to relinquish its claim and grant self-determination to the inhabitants. However, Morocco, under King Hassan II, now claimed Spanish Sahara. Algeria, barely contiguous, supported (and dominated) a Saharan independence organization called the Polisario Front. To press his claim, King Hassan organized a peaceful invasion of the disputed territory by some 350,000 Moroccans, timed to occur shortly before the Spanish withdrawal. (By contrast, the entire population of Spanish Sahara was only about 75,000.)   The United Nations called for a referendum of the Saharan population's wishes, and shortly before the Moroccan march, Spanish forces set up a "line of dissuasion" made of barbed wire and minefields some eight miles inside Spanish Sahara. Nevertheless, Hassan led hundreds of thousands of Moroccans over the border, halting them a couple of miles short of the minefields. This action was entirely peaceful, although elsewhere small Moroccan armed units clashed with Polisario Front guerrilla fighters. In the West, some media drew attention to the king's innovative methods.

The king then withdrew his 350,000 peaceful invaders, and a few days later it was announced that Morocco and Spain had come to an agreement. Under the terms, Morocco would take over control of the Spanish Sahara as Spain withdrew; in return Spain would continue to enjoy some important mineral rights in the territory. (Some observers felt that this outcome, and not the granting of national independence, was what Spain had really wanted all along.) Algeria's furious protests and the UN's appeal for a referendum were ignored, and there was some additional fighting between Moroccan troops and Algerian-supported Polisario Front guerrillas before Morocco succeeded in taking full control.

This example is a difficult one for many advocates of peace. Among others is the objection that the International Court of Justice had ruled that there was no basis in law for Morocco's claims to the Spanish Sahara. Yet the transition was accomplished without the war that many experts expected at the time.   The case demonstrates how the goal of preserving peace may conflict with other meritorious goals such as national self-determination and independence and a respected international law system.

The second case involved Goa, a small enclave on the southwestern coast of India long held by Portugal. In the years following Indian independence from the British Empire, agitation developed within India for the return of Goa. In 1955, on the eighth anniversary of Indian independence, several thousand unarmed Indians attempted a peaceful invasion of Goa. They were met by police backed by Portuguese troops, who repelled them with gunfire. Twenty-one people were killed and over one hundred were wounded. Subsequently the Indian Parliament, which had not officially backed the peaceful invasion but also had not prohibited it, banned any further such attempts.

Diplomatic efforts, already under way, were continued, with no rapid results. Finally, in 1961 the Indian government simply took over Goa with a straightforward military invasion. The territory was captured quickly with only a few casualties. (The major Western powers—spurred by Portugal, a member of NATO—introduced a resolution into the UN Security Council calling for a prompt withdrawal of the Indian troops. The resolution was quickly vetoed by the Soviet Union.)

Some commentators termed the 1955 peaceful invasion a test of nonviolent action. If so, it would seem at first glance that the test failed. But at least three further remarks could be made. In the first place, it is likely that the Indian government prohibited further peaceful invasions, after the first effort was repulsed, not only on grounds of humanitarianism or international law (as publicly stated), but also because the government knew that it had overwhelming local military superiority and was reserving the option of using that superiority later if necessary. The nonviolent option was assessed, in other words, in a context in which violence was seen as a permissible, even likely, alternative. Secondly, the nonviolent effort immediately triggered calls within Pakistan to use the same technique against Indian-held Kashmir. Perhaps the Indian government was just as happy to see the effort end in bloody failure. Thirdly, the peaceful invasion was held without television images of the clash being beamed into living rooms around the world, as could easily occur today. World opinion, therefore, was not aroused against Portugal in the same way that it might be today.

The Spanish Sahara and the Goa examples differ in some important ways. The latter was a failure and the former a success in avoiding overt military action. Also, the Spanish Sahara case is one of action by a nation-state (Morocco), while the peaceful invaders of Goa were *not* organized by a nation-state.

The possibility of peaceful invasions by groups not organized or directed by a national government is an interesting example of action at a level below the nation-state. While probably not adequate by themselves to preserve peace in many cases, such actions could make a contribution toward the effectiveness of a larger conflict resolution system. Other kinds of action at this level have also been suggested.

One such possibility is the creation of forums other than official bodies in which disputes could be explored. Perhaps model resolutions of local conflicts might be worked out in simulated negotiations between unofficial representatives of the disputants and then presented to the national governments. One might also speculate about creating some highly public (perhaps televised) but unofficial international forum in which disputes could be aired and debated for the "global village."[5]

It is also possible to theorize about the creation of settings in which large numbers of the social elites on each side of a dispute would be exposed to the opposing viewpoint, under circumstances where they felt psychologically "safe" and hence more able to "hear" a position different from their own. This idea has been suggested, for instance, as an approach to the Israel-Palestine issue. Perhaps large numbers of unofficial mediators could travel around Israeli and Palestinian areas, talking with local leaders. Or conceivably, local leaders could be transported to a distant and "safe" region such as Europe or United States for discussions.

Proposals along these lines presuppose (as many social and humanistic psychologists do) that the ostensible issue over which conflict takes place is significantly less important than the accumulation of hatreds, misperceptions, and misunderstandings on both sides. Hence if these can be worked through, the issue should be resolvable by good negotiation. This premise may fit in some cases, such as the Israeli-Palestinian conflict, and not in others. In both the Spanish Sahara and Goa cases misperception or traditional hatreds did not play a very large role. Both cases involved a situation in which a disputed territory was neither divisible nor governable jointly; there were few if any misunderstandings.

Another, more radical approach to conflict resolution by nonnational actors is the insertion of unofficial peacekeeping forces. Suppose, for instance, that the 350,000 Moroccans had been met at the border by 100,000 unarmed people who were not Spanish, Saharan, or Algerian but who had arrived to promote the UN call for a referendum among the Saharans. Probably the outcome would have been different. But this scenario has many problems. The difficulty of finding so many civilian volunteers and supporting them is obvious. More important, how could they get there without the active cooperation of the

Spanish? If the Spanish really wanted a pro-Moroccan outcome, such cooperation would not necessarily be forthcoming.

Despite such questions, the image of unofficial peacekeepers has appeal. A number of variations might be imagined. Perhaps some conflicts could be resolved through a peaceful trial of strength. Suppose, for instance, that there is a dispute between two countries about the border between them. If appeals to international law, advanced mediation techniques, and other methods have all failed, nations could demonstrate their resolve in a nonmilitary way. The civilian populace on each side might mass in the border area. If many more people turned out on one side than on the other, proving that the population on that side cared more deeply, that side would "win." If the two countries were very uneven in the size of their domestic populations, perhaps some other test than numbers could be devised. In any case, the ruling principle would be that some peaceful trial of strength would substitute for a military encounter. Other means for reducing and resolving conflicts short of war might be possible, of which the path of nonviolence (civilian-based defense) can be seen as one.

To sum up, traditional mechanisms for resolving the inevitable conflicts that arise between nations have repeatedly failed at their appointed task of reaching resolution by means short of a military trial of strength. Conflict resolution theorists conclude from this not that conflict resolution is impossible but that new and better "technology" for accomplishing it needs to be devised. Usually they hold that newer means should supplement rather than compete with the older methods. Proposed means must exclude violence but may include force and nonviolent coercion. The goal of this approach is for the means of conflict resolution to be continually developed, expanded, and improved, so that war is used less and less as a way of dealing with conflict and eventually not used at all. War would not so much be abolished as progressively rendered inferior and unacceptable.

Due to the significant shift in attitudes that the replacement of war by peaceful conflict resolution devices involves, there is a certain overlap between this approach and the last of our nine paths to peace. Let us turn to that last path, and then consider the intersection of the two together.

The Path of Changing Attitudes: The Delegitimation of War

This last path is different from all the others because it applies to attitudes and beliefs rather than to behavior. Based on psychology, it can be combined with the paths that focus on politico-military matters to yield a comprehensive approach to peace. Path nine essentially consists of withdrawing the legitimacy from war. As a growing number of nations regard war and preparation for war as legitimate under fewer and fewer circumstances, wars will become rarer. The logical endpoint of this progression is that there will be *no* circumstances under which war will be seen as legitimate, and hence wars will not recur. Although this endpoint seems a radical possibility to many, there is nothing radical about the idea that the progression can occur. In fact, in some important respects it is already occurring. There is good evidence of a long-term trend to delegitimize war.

One aspect of this trend involves people's attitudes toward offense and defense. Until at least 1914, offensive war was generally considered permissible and legitimate, at least under certain conditions. Certainly some of the European nations had fought wars that were frankly offensive in purpose. After World War I this attitude began to weaken, although it lingered to some extent as late as World War II. As noted before, since midcentury almost every military engagement around the world has been justified on defensive grounds.

It is easy to be cynical about the significance of this change. After all, much offense is justified as being defense. Nonetheless, this change in language reflects a deep and general shift in public attitudes and some attempt to limit warlike behavior. For example, old-fashioned "gunboat diplomacy," in which powerful, technically advanced nations intervened militarily in the affairs of weak Third World nations, can no longer be undertaken without immense outcry and is now rarely attempted.

That this shift is real and important can best be seen in the fact that it is continuing, deepening, and having an increasingly constraining effect. The U.S. war in Vietnam represented a crucial step in this process. Prior to that war, the U.S. could justify warfare even at a great distance on defensive grounds. This was the essence of the so-called domino theory of the Vietnam era. Better, it was said, to defend ourselves at a distance than wait for the threat to come closer to home. The domino theory was largely discredited in the course of the war and probably has been scotched completely by events since. For the United States lost the Vietnam War, but the consequences predicted by the theory did not transpire: Other nations did not topple to communism like a row of dominos. A decade after the fall of Saigon, the overall U.S. political position in Asia is as strong as, or possibly stronger than, before. As the decades pass, then, not only must defensive grounds be found for war, but the definition of legitimate defensive grounds is narrowing. There is no obvious reason that this trend should not continue.

A second respect in which war is becoming progressively delegitimized is the increasing number of areas that have achieved the state that Kenneth Boulding has called stable peace. Two nations are in "stable peace" with each other when no plausible conflict can be sufficiently intense to overcome the peaceful bonds between them. Prior to World War II it was difficult to find any major nations in this relationship other than the U.S. and Canada. Today, all of the countries of Western and neutral Europe have such relationships with each other. Japan is certainly in this relationship with both Europe and the United States, and stable peace has probably been obtained in some other significant areas in Asia. Although wide areas of the globe are not yet included, stable peace is spreading.

Yet another sign of the progressive delegitimation of war is the change in the image of military combat. There has been a shift so profound that most people now alive have forgotten what the earlier attitude was. As recently as World War I, fighting was regarded as a glorious and heroic thing to do. Especially destructive individuals were remembered by name (such as the Red Baron), and popular songs were composed about the glory and valor of the troops. But World War II produced no Red Baron, only a Kilroy who was distinguished mainly by his anonymity. We remember no heroes from Korea or Vietnam. No songs glorifying war have achieved popularity; indeed, in a generation, popular *anti*-war songs have grown more numerous. In the 1980s there is, to be sure, a trend in American cinema toward increasing, and more explicit, violence. But interestingly, this trend does not include glorification of *war*. It celebrates violent individuals, such as Rambo, but not organized warfare. This trend toward the deglorification of war can also be expected to continue.

Additional indications of the progressive delegitimation of war are found in the concern that both Americans and Europeans showed in the 1980s over the persistent threat of nuclear war. It is true that this concern has not stopped the arms race or the installation of nuclear weapons in Europe. But the half-empty glass is also half-full: It is completely unprecedented for the public to become deeply involved over the issue of a potential, as opposed to actual or imminent, war. Indeed, it is historically unprecedented for broad sectors of the public in any Western nation to take any sustained interest in peace other than in times of crisis or war.

To sum up, there is good evidence that war is gradually being seen as less and less legitimate and that this trend is likely to continue. Viewed in relation to history, this delegitimation of war is taking place with exceptional rapidity—however agonizingly slow it may appear when viewed day to day. An activity—war—that humans have engaged in enthusiastically for thousands of years has lost a surprising amount of support in only a relatively few decades.

The claim that the trend exists is relatively noncontroversial. The real debate is how far the trend can go. Skeptics claim that delegitimation will stop short of forcing the outlawing of war because war is seen as "necessary." Throughout history war has been the means of last resort for reaching a decision between two nations or groups in severe conflict. War has been the ultimate arbiter, the final way of reaching a decisive outcome (just or unjust) in cases where both sides insist on winning and only one can. The complete abolition of war cannot take place as long as there is no replacement for this ultimate arbiter.

It is at this point that conflict resolution theorists draw attention to the possibility of new, advanced conflict resolution methods. If more powerful, more effective means of resolving conflicts can be developed and become widely accepted, those means can increasingly substitute for war as a means of reaching a decision. In that event the progressive delegitimation of war can continue.

The Combination of Changing Attitudes and Alternative Conflict Resolution

We see at this point the close interrelationship between changing attitudes and new conflict resolution methods and the possibility that the two might be combined. The progressive shift in attitudes away from a belief in war requires an effective substitute for the function that war has played in resolving severe conflicts if that shift is to continue to its natural conclusion. Similarly, novel conflict resolution methods (as well as greater use of international law) will remain dreams unless public interest in and support of attempts to avoid war greatly increase. In short, changing attitudes and advanced conflict resolution methods are mutually dependent.

Humanity needs a way to resolve its serious conflicts, and war is unlikely to be abandoned until another and more acceptable way of coping with severe conflicts is developed. One of the important errors of past peace movements has been to overlook this fact. Perhaps unconsciously, these movements have tended to make the assumption that doing away with war would also mean doing away with serious human conflict and hence have paid little attention to how conflict would be resolved in the future. The Kellogg-Briand Pact was a conspicuous example. It "abolished" war without providing a substitute way of resolving conflict other than relying on existing international law, the shortcomings of which were already well known.

The main hope of many of today's peace experts lies in increasingly delegitimizing war while providing alternatives. Work is proceeding on the task of developing improved conflict resolution methods. But what can be done about attitudes? Is it simply a matter of waiting for the change to happen spontaneously, perhaps helping it a little with appropriate education?

The question is reminiscent of Lenin's problem with Marxism. Marx's theory held that industrial society inevitably shifts from capitalism to socialism and ultimately to communism—an "inevitable" trend, but undeliberate. Lenin, however, concluded that the trend should be accelerated and made deliberate; he therefore modified the theory to include the possibility that a "vanguard" could speed up the natural course of history. (Not surprisingly, he identified his own political group as the vanguard. The deliberate action chosen was the revolutionary seizure of state power.) The peace advocate who believes in the truth and importance of the long-term trend toward delegitimation of war is in an analogous position. Can the trend be accelerated by deliberate action, and if so, by what action?

There are two aspects to the answer, both important. One relates to examining and possibly changing one's own beliefs; the second involves attempting to change the beliefs of others. One may be able to convince oneself that war is already illegitimate, that sustained peace will become possible, and that the resolution without war of even severe conflicts will become possible. It is not readily apparent, in the face of strong evidence to the contrary, that this conviction would be wise. However, we do know that expectations influence perceptions; perhaps if expectations are deliberately changed, the world will change also. We will return to this subject in Chapter 5. The other aspect involves action to encourage others to make similar changes in their beliefs. The delegitimation of war does not have to proceed unconsciously and spontaneously. People can be explicitly encouraged to withdraw the legitimacy they have been granting to war.

The simplest and soundest ground on which this appeal can be based is that war has become too destructive to be countenanced. Surveys show that a large majority of the American people are now convinced of that, so far as nuclear war is concerned. But other kinds of warfare, with conventional weapons, may pose a risk of escalating into a general nuclear war—and *any* risk of such absolute destruction is unacceptable. Some people will reply that a degree of risk may have to be run unless or until an alternative to war can be found. Many sincere people who accept the need for war do so with great reluctance and only because they can conceive of no alternative. For these people, the development of powerful methods of conflict resolution might reopen an otherwise closed discussion.

Two objections to this line of thought are commonly raised. One is that there are as yet only a small number of people who are ready to declare the illegitimacy of war and these are mainly in the developed countries of the West. However, when one considers how eagerly the rest of the world seems to follow the Western cultural lead in other respects, it seems plausible that this trend too will eventually be global.

The other, more basic, objection can be put in the form of a scenario. Suppose two adjacent nations, one a democracy and the other a tyranny, are in severe conflict with each other. Suppose further that the citizens of the democracy refuse to engage in preparation for war, judging it not to be a legitimate instrument of national policy. The ruling circles of the tyranny, however, regard war as a perfectly legitimate means of seeking their own ends. All nonviolent means of conflict resolution fail to give the tyranny what it seeks. Is it not obvious that the tyranny will make war on the democracy?

This challenge admits of only two honest answers. One is that the democracy could choose the path of civilian-based defense. The other is to recognize that indeed the legitimacy cannot be fully withdrawn from war until there is sufficient global support. That conclusion does not necessarily render the entire point of view nonsensical or utopian. It has been said that nothing is more powerful than an idea whose time has come, and in modern times no sizable nation has ever succeeded for long in cutting its citizens off from the ideas current in the rest of the world. No government can begin a war and remain in power for long without the acquiescence of its citizens. A sufficiently strong trend toward delegitimizing war, then, might eventually constrain even the behavior of tyrannies.

Recapitulation

We have now described and briefly examined nine paths to peace. The results of that survey may appear disappointing in that none of the nine, nor any simple combination of them, seem likely to create a world at peace—certainly not soon. Yet the conclusion that peace cannot be achieved is not warranted.

In the introduction we advanced a concept that we called operational peace, essentially the state in which war and preparations for it are no longer legitimate and nations have limited their sovereignty sufficiently for effective peacekeeping and conflict resolution. This state would certainly *include* the goal, which humanity presumably would reach earlier, of rendering a global nuclear holocaust impossible. To reach these goals all, or nearly all, of the nine paths may play some kind of role. A shifting and evolving combination of them is probably required for any plausible scenario of the world in a state of operational peace. Let us review the nine paths from this point of view. We will first consider the approaches to achieving peace in the face of imminent or existing threat, and then all the approaches to maintaining peace.

Path one, taking direct action to remove a threat, means using military or paramilitary action. This would be considered an unattractive option by most people. When it means going to war to prevent or end a war, it is self-contradictory.

Yet even this path cannot be excluded entirely. One of the dangers that concerns thoughtful people is the possibility that a terrorist group (or a national leader of the Khomeini/Khadaffi/Idi Amin type) could come into possession of nuclear weapons. Direct action to eliminate such a threat might well win the support of many. Direct action would be particularly legitimate if it could be taken by a group of nations—or perhaps some future international body—acting for the benefit of the world. If proliferation of nuclear weapon capability continues (as it seems likely to), such direct action may prove necessary at some point along the way to operational peace.

For the moment we pass over path two, deterrence, which poses many troubling and complicated issues.

Path six, alternative defense, and path seven, nonviolent resistance, resemble each other in important ways. They differ fundamentally in their attitude toward violence. Both seek to cope with an imminent danger of invasion by making the attacked nation "indigestible," either through perpetual resistance by an armed, fighting citizenry or through resistance employing the moral advantages and appeal of nonviolence. The threat of resistance by an entire population should deter even a powerful aggressor. (This kind of deterrence, unlike nuclear deterrence, poses no threat to any third party or to the world, and hence it meets the usual criteria for legitimacy.)

As discussed earlier, there are several reasons to doubt the feasibility of either of these paths taken by itself as a general approach to achieving peace. But if accompanied by a considerable degree of disarmament, they could be much more convincing. Imagine, for instance, a world of the not-distant future in which only small, residual ("second-strike deterrent") nuclear forces remained, nations having forsaken powerful offensive conventional forces. Under those circumstances either alternative defense or nonviolent resistance could act as a strong preventive to invasion.

Continuing evolution toward a state of operational peace would make nonviolent resistance increasingly preferred over alternative defense, as the latter still involves substantial preparations for warfare. It is not hard to imagine that in a largely disarmed world in which even minor warfare had become rare, many nations might be defending themselves by a nonviolence strategy. In fact, the complete abandonment of arms in favor of such a strategy might well be an intrinsic part of the developing operational peace. It would be hard to consider life fully peaceful while whole populations were preparing for warfare, however defensive. At the same time, it would be too much to expect that any nation would give up all possibility of self-defense as long as any potential threat remained.

In the much nearer term, there is another, milder form of alternative defense that merely amounts to shifting a country's military posture to one that can effectively defend but not attack. As an early step on the road to peace, this makes sense.

All of these paths involve deterrence of one kind or another, but what shall we say of path two, which is the deterrence of attack by threatening overwhelming punishment to the attacker? The essence of this path is the threat to destroy the attacker even if one is destroyed oneself—in our era, by nuclear holocaust.

Many experts believe that a great world war between the U.S.-led and Soviet-led camps, involving many millions of deaths, would have taken place sometime during the past three or four decades had it not been for the universal fear of nuclear war. This is a proposition that can neither be proved nor refuted; regrettably, the history of the first half of this century lends it a certain plausibility.

Yet the counterpoised deterrent threats of mutual annihilation, East and West, have placed our entire civilization in jeopardy. Many people realized this afresh in the early 1980s and subjected the strategy of deterrence to a new scrutiny. Different conclusions were drawn in different quarters, but if one could identify a consensus view among those concerned over the danger of nuclear war, it might be this: The deterrence policy cannot be jettisoned overnight, but neither can it be allowed to remain the linch-pin of the international order indefinitely. Too many ways can be identified in which it could break down—through technical accident, miscalculation, or runaway escalation in a crisis.

The search is on, therefore, for ways to lessen the risks posed by deterrence as quickly as possible and to move away from reliance upon it in the longer run. It is hard to see how, barring very drastic global events, the world could move away from reliance on nuclear deterrence quickly, but establishing a *positive* direction of movement is important. During a period in which both the arms race and mutual hostilities were becoming more moderate and the U.S. and the USSR were seeking negotiated understandings, deterrence would presumably still be the bedrock of military relationship between the superpowers. This state seems to be an essential waystation on the path toward still further reduction and eventual elimination of our dependence on deterrence.

Let us turn to the five approaches intended to maintain and strengthen an existing peace. All five can—and probably should—be pursued simultaneously; they are not mutually competitive.

Path three, preventive diplomacy, applies primarily to the short to medium term, whereas path five seeks to forestall the emergence of conditions that would likely lead to future wars. Clearly, neither path has proven very successful thus far (although it must be said that path five has not been given enough resources to prove itself). It is easy to be cynical about both; diplomacy aimed at preventing war often fails, and relatively poor nations often squander a hefty portion of the aid they receive on weapons and war. Yet both paths have had their successes too. Even in the Middle East, with its venomous hatreds, diplomacy has prevented several wars in recent decades. Perhaps the easiest way to recognize the significance of path five is to imagine how dark would be the future of many areas of the world if all real effort to heal the underlying causes of war was withdrawn. Both paths need to be pursued vigorously.

With a shift in attitudes toward the further delegitimation of war, both paths might be much more promising. Diplomacy might be able to better employ a needed tool that it presently can rarely use—the appeal to world opinion. More widespread interest in sustaining peace would also direct more attention to the basic causes of war and thus reveal the need to resolve deep injustices such as the chasm between the rich North and the impoverished South.

Great reductions in arms and considerable improvement in the means of resolving conflict are as essential to operational peace as resolving the North-South dilemma is. Path four, arms control and disarmament, may seem to be accomplishing little (although the SALT agreements did create certain valuable restraints and the Non-Proliferation and Limited Test Ban treaties have helped greatly). But this path cannot be avoided. Large-scale nuclear disarmament must be a component of any lasting solution to the nuclear dilemma. Substantial reduction of offensive *conventional* capabilities would make possible a general adoption of defensive postures with their accompanying enormous reduction in threat and increase in true security.

Path eight, developing improved methods of conflict resolution, may seem—and probably is—of marginal applicability so long as reaching a decision by war continues to be acceptable. But the central insight of the conflict resolution advocates cannot be dismissed: Many sincere people reluctantly accept war as a means of reaching decision because they cannot find another means; if another effective means evolves, the progressive delegitimation of war is likely to continue. Improved conflict resolution will not consist of a single strategy any more than war involves a single strategy. International law may play a more important role; mediation and related techniques will probably play an enlarged role as well. Innovative techniques for using force nonviolently may well evolve and gather public support.

Finally, path nine, the long-term trend toward the delegitimation of war, is an essential component in achieving a peaceful world, and actively furthering that trend is an important path to peace. The belief that war is not a legitimate or necessary means of resolving serious conflicts stands in a "ratcheting" relationship to most of the paths to peace that we have discussed; the belief is both a precondition for and a result of progress on those paths. Because path nine is likely to be the least familiar and because of its importance, we will explore it further in the next chapter.

A progression from the present state of the world to one of operational peace is likely to include some contribution from all nine paths. Not all are equally important, and the paths that involve the threat to use violence (one, two, and six) will need to decline in importance and eventually fade away as the goal of operational peace approaches. Other paths, such as alternative conflict resolution and nonviolence, play little role in today's world but are likely to become increasingly important in the future. The question of a progression toward a world at peace is an important one. Indeed, an image of how that progression could prove possible is so significant a matter that we devote much of the final chapter to it.

5

The Possibility of Peace

Up to this point we have been descriptive and analytical. We have sketched the nine main paths to peace that have been tried or recommended, mentioned some of their pros and cons, and suggested that an evolving combination of most or all of them is needed if peace is to be attained. In this last chapter we step back from the trees to look at the whole forest. We assess humanity's contemporary situation more broadly and ask: What *are* the prospects for peace and what do we recommend to make those prospects brighter?

Degrees of Peace

Perhaps the easiest place to enter this complex question is to repeat our earlier observation that peace is a matter of degree. It is no compromise to admit this. Indeed it is an error to argue, as some do, that because the world is not entirely at peace, peace does not exist.

It is often overlooked that the world of the 1980s, for all its violence, is not as war-torn as it has been at previous times. We noted that certain areas appear to have achieved a stable peace that did not exist in those areas as recently as a few decades ago. In spite of the Iran-Iraq war, various Mideast wars, and the strife in Vietnam,

Afghanistan, and elsewhere, the total number of people killed in warfare in the thirty-six years since the middle of the century is far fewer than the number killed in warfare in the thirty-six years preceding midcentury.

However, these facts have not caused people to feel reassured for two main reasons. One is that television has brought the grim and bloody reality of wars into people's living rooms in a way unprecedented in history. The conventional wars of today are no more hellish than they ever were, but now far more people can experience their hellishness. (Also modern warfare directly involves civilians rather than soldiers only.) The impact of television is one of the powerful forces behind the progressive delegitimation of war—and hence is one of the hopeful portents of future peace. The other major reason people do not feel reassured by the apparent recent decrease in warfare is the danger of a global nuclear war. Vast numbers of people are aware of this danger, and their state of fear could hardly be called "peace" even if no actual fighting were going on anywhere.

In the Introduction we suggested three types of peace that humanity could strive for. In the order of ascending ambitiousness (which probably is also the chronological order in which they might be achieved) they are

- Rendering a nuclear holocaust impossible;
- Operational peace: essentially the delegitimation of war and the creation of effective conflict resolution methods;
- Complete peace: elimination of major conflict on the planet.

Each one includes and subsumes the previous one(s). Each is meant in the sense of a *sustainable* condition. (Obviously none of the three would mean much if it lasted only a few years.) Let us pause for a moment on each.

Rendering a global holocaust impossible is a goal with its own unique importance and urgency. As Jonathan Schell and many others have pointed out, preventing the absolute destruction of civilization is a moral imperative transcending all others. It is primarily the danger of destruction, and the imperative of abolishing the danger, that in our time has drawn great numbers of people into a search for peace.

Operational peace includes but goes well beyond the abolition of the global holocaust danger. It can be defined by three ingredients:

1. The delegitimation of war and preparation for war as instruments of national policy;
2. The delegitimation of all weapons of mass slaughter;

3. Sufficient limitations on national sovereignty to give effectiveness to institutions for peacekeeping and nonviolent conflict resolution.

It is probably something like this that most people have in mind when they imagine what a world at peace would mean.

Complete peace represents the logical endpoint of the progression. A world at complete peace would be a world in which all relationships were like the West European and U.S.-Canadian relationships now: A general atmosphere of good will prevails; people feel a sense of unity with one another; and conflicts can be solved by institutions for peacekeeping and nonviolent conflict resolution. For many people, this condition is imaginable for the whole world only as occurring after nation-states no longer exist as sovereign entities.

All three levels must be considered for a comprehensive view of the subject of peace. However, as we indicated in the Introduction, we believe it most important in these critical times to focus on the first two (in a way that is compatible with the eventual goal of complete peace).

The Belief in Possibility

If one is sincere in the desire for peace but also without illusions regarding the realities of contemporary international relations, the question that arises is, "On what basis is achieving these goals possible?"

A persuasive answer to this question must be found if people are to undertake effective thought and action. They cannot relate to this merely as an abstract or hypothetical question. It is not enough to believe in some intellectual sense that the goals are theoretically "possible", just as hundreds of other future states-of-the-world are imaginable and may be possible. For people to commit effort to working for peace they need to feel emotionally that peace is a *real* possibility. They must feel, "Yes, we can do that." Usually they also need to feel that it can be done within some not-too-distant time period. Though they understand that ambitious goals are not achievable quickly, the goal must not seem too remote.

We dwell on this point, which may perhaps seem obvious, for a reason: In the 1980s there is a widespread *absence* of this kind of conviction with respect to either the abolition of the global nuclear threat or to operational peace. People wish for these things, but many lack conviction that they are achievable, at least in the foreseeable future.   We believe that *the widespread absence of this belief in real possibility is one of the most important hindrances to actual progress toward these goals.*

The problem here is a circular one.   If definite and visible progress *were* being made toward these goals, the belief in their possibility would be more widespread.   That belief would in turn motivate many talented individuals to work on these challenges—the result of which would probably be further progress!   Instead, the contemporary absence of clear progress discourages individuals from such work, thus contributing to the absence of progress.   This current situation is a "vicious circle."   We will pay particular attention in this chapter to the feasibility of developing a conviction, held emotionally as well as intellectually, that we really can achieve peace—thus converting the "vicious circle" to a "virtuous circle."   The presence of such a belief would motivate serious, optimistic, forward-looking work that could accomplish much.

Toward the Belief in Possibility

How might a real belief in the possibility of peace be attained? Most people seem to need an *image* of how peace could be achieved. Theories or ideas—about, say, a future world system—are not enough. General concepts such as our nine paths to peace are not enough.   People need a "picture" of the world in the not-distant future that shows, concretely, the goal achieved or being achieved.   Experimentation shows that a plausible image of a task accomplished or being accomplished is much more powerful in convincing people of the real possibility than theories and concepts alone are.

As one researcher explains the effect of this image, "People who have felt helpless in the face of the nuclear confrontation between the superpowers and for whom a weapon-free world simply is not thinkable have found themselves not only able to picture a demilitarized social order, but to visualize strategies they never thought of before to achieve it."[6]

A common approach in this research is to suggest that individuals or groups develop an image for the world of, say, two or three decades hence, in which (for example) the goal of rendering a global nuclear holocaust impossible has been achieved.   The question might then be posed, "How was this accomplished?"

Two important balances are essential to the credibility of the image. First, this image need not be complete in its details.   People understand that not every question can be, or needs to be, answered now.   Indeed, complete plans for world peace arouse well-justified skepticism. Furthermore, an image that too specifically presents just *one* way to peace would exclude other ways that might be valuable. On the other hand, the image cannot be too vague either; telling people "Just imagine that there are some working peacekeeping institutions in existence" is hardly helpful. A useful image needs to be somewhat concrete but should be a sketch rather than a plan.

Second, a useful image needs to strike a balance between being too close and being too remote, both in time and in the magnitude of changes involved. The image must be far enough in the future that people can believe that important changes in the world could occur by then. Drastic changes in a single decade, for instance, might indeed occur but the likelihood is not great enough to be persuasive. Yet the image must also be close enough to be seen as relevant. Images that project far into the future or that picture a world too radically different from ours are not convincing. For example, most people feel that the state of the world a century from now cannot be predicted or imaged accurately. Similarly, few find persuasive an image of the near-future world that is unrecognizably different from the present world. For instance, hardly anyone in the late 1980s can believe in a world in the year 2000 in which nation-states had been abolished in favor of a single, benevolent world government patterned on Western constitutional democracies.

To conclude, *an essential task in achieving peace is the creation, and propagation to a wide audience, of a credible image of a peaceful future.* Such an image could be a source of hope for great numbers of people who presently have little hope for future peace and could help motivate many individuals to work toward achieving peace.

The importance of developing such an image has been noted by others. As of this writing, the best-known example is the contest conducted in the spring of 1985 by *The Christian Science Monitor*. The newspaper invited its readers to submit essays picturing a world at peace twenty-five years in the future and describing how that world was reached. Hundreds of entries were received. The three winning essays were published in the *Monitor*, and later a whole book of these essays was published. In creating this competition, the *Monitor* editors were responding to the striking lack of any convincing image of a future world at peace.[7]

The *Monitor's* scenarios differed from the positive image we seek in that the contest rules allowed scenarios in which peace is achieved by way of large-scale violence and social disruption. (In fact, in one of the three winning essays peace was achieved through a worldwide reaction to a regional nuclear war in the Indian subcontinent.) One would hardly want to *plan* to achieve peace by such a route. Furthermore, such a scenario does not inspire belief that peace is achievable through committed effort because the outcome of such a war could easily be something quite different from peace. Thus a third requirement for peace images whose purpose is to stimulate belief in the possibility of peace or to motivate work toward peace is that the images substitute peaceful or less violent methods for the violent existing methods.

Let us sum up this part of our argument: A major step toward peace is the development of a convincing image of a future world at peace. There might be few greater contributions to the cause of peace than the development during the next few years of such an image in a form that would be persuasive and attractive to large numbers of people. Even if the actual future turned out somewhat differently, the spreading image could create the belief in the possibility of peace. That belief is a sine qua non of progress.

Some Elements of an Image

Creation of a powerful image should be an enterprise to which many contribute. We will not attempt to accomplish it here. We do, however, wish to suggest some possible elements of a convincing image. Later in this chapter we will also develop two powerful reasons why an image of a peaceful world may be more plausible than many presently believe.

We will use a slight modification of the imaging technique. Rather than constructing an image of a world already *fully* in the state we call operational peace, we will suggest an image of a world *well on its way* to peace. This modification is an additional idea we want to contribute to the technique. It is especially useful in this context because the goal of peace may seem to many to be extremely "far away" and difficult to achieve. A useful way around the difficulty is to choose an intermediate and more convincing goal that many will find easier to imagine. The image we advance now, therefore, is one of a world of the not-distant future well on its way to operational peace. Because different assumptions about timing will be plausible to different people and we don't want to confuse the issues by objections to the timing, we will leave indefinite the precise year of our image.

We describe it in terms of our nine paths, taken in the reverse order to the original order of presentation:

Path Nine. By this time, the majority of people in the powerful countries hold the belief that sustainable, operational peace is possible and is achievable within a reasonable time. The legitimacy of war has been effectively challenged in most countries, and the idea that limits on national sovereignty are needed if civilization is to survive is gaining support. Belief in the possibility of peace is stronger in some groups and in some parts of the world than in other groups and areas, but it is held to some extent globally and is adopted by more people each passing year, a fact that adds to its credibility and builds a momentum for further dissemination. Partly for this reason, large numbers of individuals are now working seriously and optimistically on developing ways in which peace can be achieved and sustained.

Path Eight. A variety of conflict resolution methods are now being used to head off wars. These methods include international law and newer techniques such as peaceful interventions by nongovernmental groups and some applications of nonviolent force. Conflict resolution is not invariably successful, and some warfare is still occurring. However, these methods succeed often enough that there now exists widespread confidence in their further development and more frequent success.

Path Seven. A number of nations are training their populations in the use of nonviolence in order to lessen the possibility of invasion. For certain nations, this has already become the principal means of deterring aggression; other nations are seriously considering it.

Path Six. Certain nations have decided that armed civilian resistance will be a more successful deterrent in their situation than nonviolent resistance would be. In some cases these nations are expecting to shift to nonviolent resistance later. Meanwhile many countries—particularly those that have historical or other reasons to feel especially threatened—have structured their regular military forces in postures capable only of defense. Such nonoffensive forces clearly do not threaten the peace.

Path Five. Substantial progress is being made to resolve the sources of potential wars. Some serious political conflicts, rooted in traditional hatreds and perceived injustices, still exist in certain regions, and the tremendous gap in living conditions between North and South has only been partly ameliorated. But fewer seeds of *future* violent conflicts are being sown than at any time earlier. Hence it is becoming increasingly plausible that the direction of history is toward decreasing conflict.

Path Four. Disarmament policies have not yet abolished all nuclear weapons but have drastically reduced the number of weapons to the minimal levels required to deter any rational opponent's nuclear attack. There is an almost universal consensus now that nuclear weapons are "unusable." Hence proliferation has stopped, both in nonnuclear nations and in nations already possessing nuclear weapons. Serious discussions are now underway for still further reductions and for the elimination of any remaining possibility (by now almost negligible) of an accidental or unintended nuclear war.

Path Three. Traditional preventive diplomacy has been greatly strengthened by being able to draw on the pressure of world opinion as a prevailing moral force.

Path Two. Nuclear deterrence persists only in the limited, special form just described. There are serious discussions now of creating a single global anti-ballistic missile defense shield adequate to stop nearly all of the relatively few missiles still existing. There also are many who prefer to avoid that great expense and depend instead on rapid progress toward agreement on the verified dismantling of all offensive nuclear systems.

Path One. It has been necessary on two occasions up to this time forcibly to remove nuclear weapons from the hands of dictators who might have used them. It is now thought unlikely that such an action will ever be necessary again. One of the two dictators found himself ousted as a by-product of the action.

We believe that this is a plausible image for the not-distant future. Each of the elements taken by itself is attainable, and because they do not conflict—indeed they reinforce one another—the world they create when combined is also attainable. It is a world of much greater peace than our present one, a world well on its way to full operational peace. As we indicated, this is far from a complete image; many other elements may be needed for the complete and plausible image that we believe is necessary. We have only summarized what each of the nine paths discussed in this book might contribute at an imagined future time.

The Importance of Attitudes

Whether the world just described can be achieved depends on a number of factors, of which perhaps none is more important than the attitudes of people worldwide. The most crucial contribution to this future world is that of path nine. As we have stressed in this chapter, the kinds of progress that this image illustrates are unlikely to be realized unless large numbers of people come to believe in the real possibility of peace and a significant number become willing to work to achieve that goal.

The belief that real peace is possible is both a precondition for and a result of progress toward peace. It is an essential *precondition* for serious, sustained effort of any kind. Whether the work is toward disarmament, toward the delegitimation of war, toward amelioration of the underlying causes of war, toward defensive nonthreatening postures, or toward better conflict resolution, people must believe not only that peace is strengthened thereby but that the long-term direction of history is toward peace (even if there is some backward as well as forward movement along the way). The belief is also a *result* because some progress—often even small progress—makes the belief still more convincing to those who hold it and makes it credible to more people. For any of these paths to contribute to the credibility of eventual peace the path need not invariably succeed, provided that good reasons can be found why failures occur and why improvements can promise better results in the future.

The Realism of Believing in Peace

Belief in the possibility of peace is not unrealistic. People who are skeptical about peace often claim that it is, and say that their "realism" is based on a reading of history. They claim that because humanity has nearly always been engaged in wars it will continue to be. But this is not the only "realistic" way to look at the question; in fact, in the end it may be less realistic than some alternative.

Historically speaking, it is not in fact true that humanity has nearly always been engaged in wars. According to the archeological evidence, warfare scarcely existed among any known tribe or group prior to approximately 5000 B.C. Sometime around this date, war was "invented." If there was a time in humanity's past when war did not exist, it is not unrealistic to imagine a time in its future when war again does not exist. However, as long as we can only theorize about why war was invented some 7,000 years ago, this historical fact, while significant, is not directly useful.

Another not very useful idea that is sometimes put forth in favor of the plausibility of peace is that the realization of how destructive nuclear weapons are "simply must" awaken humanity to the senselessness of war. Similar arguments were advanced with the inventions of dynamite, the machine gun, and the airplane. Apparently human beings are not easily swayed by this logic.

There are, however, two powerful reasons for believing that a continuation of "warfare as usual" is *not* the only realistic expectation and may indeed be less realistic than a more optimistic view. The reasons involve topics that may seem far removed from the matters we have been concerned with until now but actually are not. The first has to do with developments in the understanding of the human psyche and consciousness. The second relates to certain characteristics of broad, fundamental societal change.

The Power of Understanding the Psyche

"Since wars are born in the minds of men," states the Preamble to the UNESCO Charter, "it is in the minds of men where we have to erect the ramparts of peace."

In recent decades, psychologists and other researchers of the human mind have been making important advances in understanding the roots of war—advances that are continuing and perhaps accelerating. These have not yet seen the kinds of applications to peace issues that probably will bear much fruit in the future. There is an excellent reason to think that an era of powerful understanding and potent tools is now dawning. To do justice to this progress and offer an adequate appraisal of it would be far beyond the scope of this book, but we will sketch the avenues, mention briefly why they are promising, and indicate some further useful reading.

The full power of what understanding of the psyche can offer can only be appreciated if the various strands of that understanding are grasped as a whole. But it is useful to separate the strands in a quick survey like this one, keeping in mind these intermingled approaches overlap each other. Three classes of insights can be usefully distinguished: those belonging to social and cognitive psychology, those of depth psychology (including psychoanalysis), and those of contemporary research on consciousness.

The class involving social and cognitive psychology has its roots in the empirical, experimental tradition. The insights especially relevant to peace arise from research on *perception* and *attribution*. How do we perceive the outer world, especially other persons, and why do our perceptions sometimes differ from those of others—and from reality? What do we attribute to others—that is, what motivations do we assume in them, and what explanations do we come up with for their behavior? How does cognitive functioning restrict people's abilities to comprehend complexity and to achieve what is in their own best interests? There is an enormous body of research on these kinds of questions, some of which is highly applicable to peace. In important respects the behavior of nations resembles the behavior of individuals, and research on the latter sheds light on the former. A few elementary examples will illustrate the applicability:

- In complex situations involving two parties, each of which perceives the other's overall goals to be threatening or illegitimate, each party is likely to interpret ambiguous behavior by the other as hostile. Behavior suggesting aggressiveness is more noticeable than behavior suggesting peaceableness, and once noticed, the former is likely to be interpreted in the most hostile terms that the evidence can reasonably sustain;

- In situations of mutual antagonism, each hostile act by one party tends to reinforce the other's perception of hostility. As a consequence of repeated reinforcement, a strong expectation of hostility may be built up. Peaceful initiatives then must overcome entrenched attitudes, which can often be done only with great difficulty;
- Cognitive limitations on information processing tend to produce images of the other party that are considerably oversimplified versions of the reality. In an emotional context of anxiety, the simplifications made will be those consistent with fear;
- Costly or difficult actions that one takes in the name of defense tend to reinforce one's presumption that the other party is hostile because it becomes too emotionally difficult to admit to oneself that one's assumptions might have been wrong and that all that cost may have been unnecessary;
- Aggressive individuals who have climbed to the top in highly competitive government hierarchies are likely to attribute aggressive characteristics to their counterparts in other government hierarchies;
- Entrenched perceptions and attitudes become part of national leaders' and whole populations' definitions of reality. Perceptions become so interwoven with the entire "inner map" of the--way-things-are that they become very difficult to change.

Such ideas arising from empirical research (presented here in simplified form) shed much light on international behavior. Although they do not lead to easy answers for creating peace, their accumulated power can add up to an enormously potent diagnosis of situations where peace is threatened. An accurate diagnosis can tell us in which directions work to change the situation can be most effective and should be pursued, as well as which directions are likely to be least effective. In some cases, the converse of the ideas are equally true and can help sustain peace. For example, two nations in a long-standing state of stable peace remain so in part because *peaceful* expectations have become interwoven into leaders' and populations' definitions of reality.

The second class of insights, which to some extent overlaps the first, is drawn from the tradition of *depth psychology,* which includes psychoanalysis. While not empirical in the strict sense, this tradition is based on clinical observation and disciplined introspection and can provide some highly provocative ideas. Perhaps the most important contribution from this tradition is the insight that people do not necessarily want peace. More precisely, they may unconsciously not want peace even though consciously they think they do.

Although this idea (like many from depth psychology) appears to fly in the face of common sense, there is enormous evidence for it. In somewhat different ways, the various schools of depth psychology all point to a near-universal phenomenon of profound conflicts hidden within the individual psyche—of the psyche "at war" with itself. Although technically a metaphor, this statement well describes the inner situation. There must be a profound link between the "war" or near-war that occurs deep in the inner psyches of millions of individuals and the actual wars that are fought at the level of external behavior. One of the fundamental premises of depth psychology is that inner conflicts are sooner or later acted out in behavior, although not necessarily in directly related ways. (This characteristic may provide an important key for international peace, as the externalization can take the form of *symbolic* behavior.)

Of the many rich implications that the depth-psychological perspective can suggest, the most disturbing for many advocates of peace is the idea that war and destruction appeal to some people. People do not usually acknowledge the attraction consciously, but the indirect evidence is clear. A more accurate—and for some, even more disturbing—way to say it is that at a deep level *everyone* to some extent finds war and destruction attractive.

Uncomfortable as this perspective may seem, its potential value as a tool for getting to the roots of peace and war could be enormous. The presence of unconscious motivation does not mean that the whole world must be psychoanalyzed before peace can be attained, but some principles of statecraft may need to be adjusted, and some new or newly modified forms of symbolic behavior may need to be found. It is a fundamental principle of depth psychology that motives that are brought to the surface, acknowledged, and worked with can usually be controlled, whereas the motives we do not know about or refuse to acknowledge control us.

The third class of insight, which overlaps the second, derives from research on *consciousness*. Again, this is a field that is not experimental but that does include a richness of systematic observation that can provide extremely useful insight. Perhaps the most consequential finding from this research is the discovery of the startling extent to which our perceptions, motivations, values, and behaviors are shaped by *unconscious beliefs*—or, to employ a computer metaphor, by "unconscious programming." Acting at an unconscious level, these beliefs are largely acquired through our interpretations of early experiences and from the cultural milieu. These beliefs are relatively inaccessible to conscious awareness, and their existence is inferred largely from observation of behavior. The link to behavior is apparent for such example beliefs as "I am inadequate," "The world is hostile," "People with skin of a different color are alien," and so forth.

Research shows that the power of this programming is awesome. For instance, anthropologists find that individuals who are raised in different tribal cultures literally perceive different realities. They do not just believe in different ideas; they experience a different world. The most honest reports from a tribe member describe a reality that is in important respects quite different from that seen by someone from another culture (such as the anthropologist). One can only conjecture the extent to which collective unconscious beliefs may affect the perceptions and performance effectiveness of whole societies.

To an extent that is still unknown but may be very great, unconscious programming can be altered by deliberate counterprogramming. Some practical examples of this principle are now widely accepted. Many athletic coaches, for instance, now include exercises in inner imaging or "affirmation" in their training regimes. Imaging and affirmation are visual and verbal forms of the same process: A new belief is accepted and repeated consciously, as a way of "reprogramming" the unconscious mind. Someone who is learning to pole-vault, for instance, may be given the exercise of visualizing himself vaulting higher than he yet has, visualizing this as vividly as possible and "feeling" the experience in his body. Soon what is so vividly imaged becomes true in experience. This approach has also been widely accepted in the world of U.S. business. Numerous training programs, workshops, and executive seminars train salespeople to visualize breaking past sales records, train executives persistently to affirm while in a state of deep relaxation that desired goals are already achieved, and so forth.

An exciting aspect of this approach, as of many other psychological insights, is that the limits of its applicability have not yet been found. Neither its potential scope nor its power in any one sphere are yet known. Neither do we know very much yet about a possibility even more intriguing for world peace: What are the effects when the same image is affirmed by vast numbers of people? Today's widespread fear of nuclear holocaust or collective resignation over the impossibility of real peace may be having a far more profound negative effect in world affairs than has yet been appreciated. Similarly, a spreading belief in the achievability of peace might have positive effects that would go far beyond the obvious generation of hope and motivation.

Thus some or all of the psychological conditions that hinder peace— hostile expectations, unconscious attractions to conflict, and so on—may be overcome more readily by techniques for the affirmation and imaging of peace than by rational persuasion. Or other psychological discoveries still awaiting us may interconnect with the insights of social and cognitive psychology, of depth psychology, and of consciousness research.

How can we arrive at a balanced assessment of what these approaches can offer? Some among the educated public feel a certain skepticism about the psychological approaches to peace issues. This skepticism arises from an impression that excessive claims have sometimes been made for these approaches and from a suspicion that the principles of individual psychology do not translate in any simple way to the collective dynamics of great masses of people. It is true that psychologists in recent decades have sometimes found that simple applications of their principles did not successfully address the power and complexity of relations among nations. Occasional claims that psychological understandings could quickly resolve the problem of war have proven exaggerated. It is important that the applicability of these approaches be neither oversold nor undersold and that they be assessed on the basis of consistent results.

An antidote to both premature claims and backlash disappointments is to take a longer-range view. Research on the human psyche is a young science, both in absolute terms and even more so in relation to the depth and richness of the human mind. Younger still is serious research on psychological approaches to war and peace. When one views the already significant results of research in this new field against the backdrop of many centuries of human history, one is impressed by not how little has been accomplished but how much. The combined power of several psychological approaches, properly synthesized and applied, can add up in a reasonable time to progress of breakthrough proportions.

An illustration that shows both the relevance and the limitations of the psychological/consciousness approach is provided by Stanley Hoffman's 1985 presidential address to the International Society of Political Psychology. In commenting on the application of this approach to the problem of war, Hoffman used the example of the Warsaw Uprising of 1944. At the time of the uprising, the Soviet counterattack against the Nazi invasion had reached the vicinity of Warsaw, but the Soviets halted for a period while the Nazi occupiers of the city seized their final opportunity to exterminate the city's Jews. The Jewish population rose up in self-defense and heroically resisted the Nazi war machine by every possible means until nearly all the Jews were slaughtered or carried away to the extermination camps.

Hoffman's point is a double-edged one. The psychological/ consciousness approaches can probably yield significant results when

ERRATA

On page 86, "Hoffman" should be spelled "Hoffmann."

On page 86, line 6 of the last full paragraph, "1944" should be "1943." The next sentence should be deleted. At the end of the same paragraph, this sentence should be added: The following year the Soviet Army, nearing Warsaw, halted for a period, while the Nazi occupiers wiped out Polish resistance forces that had revolted openly as the Soviets approached.

applied to the question of why the Soviets stopped near Warsaw and can certainly yield vital insights into why the Nazis fought the Jews in Warsaw and into the roots of Nazi behavior in general. But there is something inherently objectionable in the very idea that the rules and principles of psychology and consciousness should be applied to "explain" why the Jews fought the Nazis.

This example clarifies the true power and promise of the psychological/consciousness approaches. Fully developed and applied, these approaches may help prevent war, or war-prone situations, from arising in the first place. They can create "situations of healing," in which seeds like Nazi violence are not planted or if planted never sprout. However, they may not be very applicable or appropriate to specific situations like the one that faced the Warsaw Jews once conflict has materialized. They also are not very useful when applied only to one side in an actual or potential conflict. Consider, for instance, the U.S.-Soviet nuclear arms race. To apply a psychological approach to one side only will be useless or misleading—the behavior of either side can be understood only in terms of the interaction of both sides.

The possibility that psychological approaches may be oversimplified or misapplied does not mean that these approaches are invalid. Similar limitations have often been found when fresh techniques or "young" sciences have been applied to any kind of problem. In the long run, the promise of psychological approaches to peace, appropriately refined and developed, is enormous.

The developing power of the psychological/consciousness approaches to peace issues is one of two important though often unappreciated grounds for a realistic belief in the possibility of permanently sustainable peace. The second is the host of contemporary indications of fundamental societal change.

The Plausibility of Transformative Change

The twentieth century will almost certainly turn out to be a pivotal one in human history. One indication of this is of course its vast range of new sciences and technologies. Another indication is the rapid and promising development of psychology and studies of human consciousness. A third indication, not often remarked until lately, is the surprisingly large number of thinkers who tell us that human affairs are soon to change profoundly.

This idea first appeared among a few of the great philosophers of the nineteenth century and has been propounded by an increasing number of social scientists, historians, artists, and philosophers in the decades since. The idea of imminent change was popularized in the "Aquarian Age" notions of the counterculture that appeared in the United States and Europe in the 1960s and in more sober form had become almost a cliché in some intellectual circles by the mid-1970s. The idea has now attained respectability across much of the intellectual spectrum as being worthy of serious attention.

The most basic form of the idea, stripped of astrological and other particularistic interpretations, is probably the best. That form says simply that human civilization is now on the threshold of a great transformation comparable to several in the past. The core concept is of an "age," as in "the modern age" or the "Middle Ages." World civilization, according to this idea, is about to shift from the modern, industrial age into another age—just as Western civilization shifted from the Middle Ages to the modern age. This coming age is often simply referred to as the "next age" or the "new age."

One should not underestimate the sweep and power of an idea that assumes that *all* aspects of social life and institutions may change profoundly. The analogy of the shift from the Middle Ages to the modern age is illuminating; almost every dimension and aspect of society was affected. The general organization of society, the structure of economies, the relationships between local and large political units, the meaning and purpose of politics, the role of religion, and many other key aspects of life and society were altered enormously between medieval times and the late seventeenth century. Implicit in the anticipation of a new age is the belief that such profound changes in human society could occur again.

Many important thinkers have predicted a transformation of this order. In the nineteenth century Hegel helped to set the stage by introducing the concept, later adopted deeply by Western culture, that history is an *evolving* force. Schopenhauer and Marx each elaborated on this concept and gave it his own particular twist. Late in the nineteenth century, Nietzsche announced that after his era, all things would be changed. Around the same time, Oswald Spengler devoted his most famous work to the historical pattern he saw emerging. Not surprisingly, he could perceive the coming end of his own era but could not yet discern the dawn of a new era. *The Decline of the West* is deeply pessimistic because Spengler perceived that all aspects of the current civilization were interwoven and hence were doomed together.

Early in this century, Arnold Toynbee carried out monumental research tracing the rise and fall of more than a score of past civilizations. On the basis of this work he too anticipated an early end to the industrial era as we have known it, and he was generally interpreted as being profoundly pessimistic about the future of modern civilization. However, he did speak of the possible transfiguration of industrial society into some kind of new, respiritualized form.

Between the two world wars, Pitirim Sorokin, a famous Harvard sociologist, wrote a four-volume work, *Social and Cultural Dynamics,* which he later summarized in *The Crisis of Our Age.* His conclusion, based on an impressive study of cultural and social indicators as far back as he could find any records, was that Western society, like some before it, had become so dominated by "sensate" values that it almost inevitably must react. He too suggested that the present period could not continue long and described signs of impending transformation.

Among the most optimistic of the transformationalist writers was Lewis Mumford. In the 1950s, in a little book entitled *The Transformations of Man,* he described previous transformations of Western civilization and outlined the new transformation he saw coming:

> Every transformation of man . . . has rested on a new metaphysical and ideological base; or rather, upon a new picture of the cosmos and the nature of man. . . . We stand on the brink of [such] a new age . . . an age of renewal . . . and a higher trajectory for life as a whole. . . . In carrying man's self-transformation to this further stage, world culture may bring about a fresh release of spiritual energy that will unveil new potentialities, no more visible in the human self today than radium was in the physical world a century ago, though always present.[8]

Since the 1960s there has been a flood of books, some of which achieved considerable fame, that propounded different aspects of the same theme. Theodore Roszak's *Person/Planet* discusses, as its subtitle says, "the creative disintegration of industrial society" into a new society. Fritjof Capra's *The Turning Point* and Morris Berman's *The Reenchantment of the World,* along with a number of other works, emphasize the radical implications of fundamental changes now occurring in the very definition of science, and the inevitable change this will mean for society. More journalistically, Alvin Toffler in *The Third Wave* proclaims boldly, "Humanity . . . faces the deepest upheaval and social restructuring of all time." And Marilyn Ferguson describes recent cultural developments in terms of fundamental societal transformation in *The Aquarian Conspiracy.* Two of the most subtle explorations of the deeper psychological and social meanings of the transformation appear in books with similar titles: *The End of the Modern Age* by Allen Wheelis and *The Passing of the Modern Age* by John Lukacs.

All these writers do not have the same views on the character of the impending changes or on how great a discontinuity may be expected between one era and the next. There are also important disagreements about values among thinkers who share a "shift in age" perspective. For example, some of them extol the liberation they believe high technology can bring, and others see technology as a villain. Despite the differences, the agreements among these writers are striking. Equally striking is how many of the best contemporary thinkers agree that something resembling a shift in eras is impending, and how few feel that things are likely to continue much longer as they are or with merely "linear" improvements. This current feeling is especially marked when compared with the attitudes of past generations: Throughout the eighteenth and nineteenth centuries most observers were anticipating "more and better of the same," and anticipations of a major discontinuity were rare.

A discontinuity in historical context does not necessarily mean a sudden disruptive break. Western civilization has gone through two great discontinuities—the end of the classical, Greco-Roman world and the end of the Middle Ages. The first (the fall of the Roman Empire) was relatively abrupt and violent: a period of internal decay followed by a rapid succession of barbarian invasions. The second was much more gradual. Depending on how one chooses to count the milestone events, the shift from the Middle Ages lasted from the beginning of the Renaissance in Italy in the late fourteenth century, through the Reformation period in Northern Europe, and well into the seventeenth century—over two centuries in all. The shift from the Middle Ages to the modern age went through at least two major transitional phases, the Renaissance and the Reformation periods.

Nearly all contemporary thinkers who anticipate some analogous shift assume that the speed of today's communications and transportation, the now greatly interconnected globe, and the general rapidity with which most change takes place in our time indicate that the transition period for the coming transformation will be short— probably measured in decades rather than centuries.

The Shape of the Next Age

What might this next age be like? And why should the fact that it is predicted add conviction to one's belief in the real possibility of peace?

For a complete answer to the first question we refer the reader to the books just mentioned and to others of the same genre. Here we will only sketch in some outlines. There seem to be two fruitful approaches to the question of the shape of the next age. One can see what some of today's advanced social trends seem to suggest, and one can examine the implications of frontier research and thinking. There is, as we shall see, a possible trap in exploring them but it is useful nonetheless. The advanced social trends of the last several decades may best be seen as making up a single whole, but five interrelated goals can be usefully distinguished.

1. *A search for wholeness.* Many people experienced contemporary life as being fragmented. Urbanization and a technical ethic of "man controlling nature" had contributed to a separation of people from biological life. The economy and economic purposes had become separate from and dominant over the rest of society in both capitalist and socialist countries. Many people's jobs were alienating in that the work was disconnected from any final product and from the rest of life. Religion too was experienced as a fragment, something performed at one place at particular times and hardly connected to one's living and actions. Several related movements arose in response: an ecological movement, a holistic health movement, an emphasis on the quality of life, an appropriate technology movement. These and other movements express the view that life should be whole and that there is something wrong with a society that breaks it into fragments.

2. *A search for community and relationship.* Urbanization and other factors had removed most jobs from home and neighborhood, and as a result many people experienced a loss of local community. Emphasis on consumption and on the pleasures that technology can bring had diminished the richness that people had previously experienced in family life and in extended families, neighborhoods, and many kinds of social groupings. For many, community and relationships had become impoverished. Important responses included much more extensive experimentation with group therapies and "mutual support" groupings. There was a rise in the informal economy, in deliberate decentralization, in reruralization and in the creation of intentional communities.

3. *A search for identity.* In reaction to the depersonalizing aspects of modern society, a widespread search for new ways to fashion personal identity developed. Many people explored personal psycho-therapies, "workshops," "seminars," and structured group therapy experiences. The "me generation" phenomenon of the 1970s has been interpreted alternatively as another manifestation or as an aberration of the contemporary search for identity. At the collective level, powerful forms of the search for identity also emerged. Ethnic groups asserted their differences: Blacks and Hispanics in the United States, Québecois in Canada, the Basques and Scots in Europe. Homosexuals

"came out of the closet" en masse and demanded to be accepted as themselves. The disabled rejected the term "cripple" and showed surprising political strength as they insisted on equal access and rights. The women's movement in its various forms emerged as one of the most extensive and profound attempts in history to redefine identity. In a slightly different sense, many Third World groups and nations are struggling to define their identity in a world that has come to judge value largely in Western terms.

4. *A search for meaning.* Western society had experienced a crisis of meaning and values. With the "great debunking" of religion by reductionistic, positivistic science and with a spreading sense that economic production, consumption, and even technological achievement were inadequate as primary sources of meaning, a vacuum was felt at the core of Western values. Some people reacted by developing an interest in Eastern philosophies and religious outlooks; some explored meditative disciplines, yoga, or mind-altering drug experiences; some were attracted to the emerging fields of humanistic and transpersonal psychology. A completely different response to the sense of inadequate meaning in contemporary values was the resurgence of Christian fundamentalism. This powerful movement can be interpreted as a reaffirmation of strongly held values that conflict with, and are believed to be far superior to, positivistic science and materialistic concerns. (Christian fundamentalism could also be further evidence that profound changes are afoot in the social order. Historical periods of change and uncertainty have often been accompanied by resurgences of some form of fundamentalism.) Thus there are many signs of a respiritualization of Western society and a search for, or reaffirmation of, values and meanings quite different from those of the mainstream secular culture.

5. *A sense of empowerment.* In the 1960s, a trend toward a popular sense of empowerment to reverse official decisions emerged. The end of U. S. involvement in the Vietnam War, for example, was advocated by large numbers of people determined to reverse official policy to which a powerful government had become deeply committed. There have, of course, been other popular movements with a sense of being empowered—the labor movement of the late nineteenth and early twentieth centuries, for instance. But what was striking about this trend was people's willingness to take on issues with a high technical or specialist content. Examples include the halt of the U.S. supersonic transport (SST), the popular resistance to nuclear power, suspicion of biotechnology, and perhaps above all, the deep and lasting public concern to protect the environment. In all these cases, popular

movements felt empowered to assert the importance of global and long-term costs over local and short-term gains.

These five aspects of contemporary social movements (with the possible exception of the element of religious fundamentalism) seem to make up a single broad development. Some of the specific movements and trends just mentioned were less evident in the 1980s than they were ten or fifteen years earlier. Others, like environmental concern, continue powerfully although their form may have changed significantly. Trends that are less immediately evident may be in the process of absorbing and consolidating past advances before pressing for new advances. Social change often occurs not in steady gains but in a two-steps-forward-one-step-back manner that allows changes to be incorporated into the social system.

The overall pattern of trends just described, which obviously includes the increasing delegitimation of war, may give some hint of future social directions. A second hint of the next age is provided by frontier research and thinking.

The last third of the twentieth century has been witnessing ferment in the epistemological roots of many sciences. Physics is the most widely discussed example. Physics has been steadily abandoning the materialistic base it had hitherto embraced in favor of an emphasis on processes. A number of writers over the past two decades have been struck by the increasing resemblance between physicists' descriptions of reality and the traditional descriptions provided by the Eastern religious philosophies. (Two of the most accessible discussions are *The Tao of Physics* by Fritjof Capra and *The Dancing Wu-Li Masters* by Gary Zukav.)

In the biological and human sciences, too, a similar ferment is developing. For example, Nobel laureate Roger Sperry, in the invited lead article for the 1981 *Annual Review of Neuroscience*, speaks of

recent changes in concepts relating to the mind of man, the nature of the conscious self, freedom of choice, causal determinacy, and . . . the fundamental relation of mind to matter and to brain mechanism. . . . Current concepts of the mind-brain relation involve a direct break with the long-established materialist and behaviorist doctrine that has dominated neuroscience for many decades. Instead of renouncing or ignoring consciousness, the new interpretation gives full recognition to the primacy of inner conscious awareness as a causal reality.[9]

Although "the primacy of inner conscious awareness as a causal reality" is a concept still far from being generally accepted by scientists, a debate has been opened that is not likely to be closed by any simple reembracing of once-axiomatic positivism.

Analogous shifts can be discerned in many sciences. In a pioneering study of this transformation, Peter Schwartz and Jay Ogilvy examined some seventeen physical, biological, and social sciences and found broadly similar changes, which they and others term "paradigm changes," occurring in fundamental conceptions. Precisely because the changes are breaking new ground, finding adequate labels to identify these shifts is not easy. In general the shifts tend to be from structure to process, from linear to multidimensional logic, from mechanistic to holographic models, from hierarchical to nonhierarchical ordering, from a focus on elements to one on "whole systems," and, most generally, from an orientation toward matter-energy to one emphasizing relationships and connections. Many scientists describe the overall transformation occurring in the roots of their disciplines as revolutionary.

The resemblance between these developments on the frontier of thought and the overall social developments previously described may not be easily nameable, but it is clear and undeniable. The fact that profound developments are occurring at the same time both in the realm of thought and in the realm of social change and that these developments resemble each other would seem to increase the significance of both. It is hard to avoid the conclusion that there must be some deep relationship between these developments and the coming shift from the modern to the next age proclaimed by so many. It is reasonable to suppose that these changes (and perhaps especially the developments in the sciences) are a kind of "leading edge" or precursor of the next age.

As noted there is a trap to be avoided in this line of reasoning. It would be a mistake to assume that there must be a *direct* relationship between these developments and the character of the next age—that is, to assume that the next era in history can be characterized by simple extrapolation of these trends.

Again the analogy with the transition from the Middle Ages to the modern age can be helpful. Imagine a perceptive observer living, say, in Italy in 1425. This person notices many signs that profound changes are beginning and he concludes, "Aha, there is a Renaissance dawning; we are in for a new age." So far so good—he would be correct, as we now know.

Now imagine further that among the social and intellectual developments noticed by our observer are two that strike him as particularly important—a sudden rise in interest in pre-Christian antiquity and a rapid growth in disposable wealth. Our observer might have been tempted to argue that the new age would be intellectually based in the pre-Christian, classical worldview. *That* prediction would have been essentially wrong. (It would have been somewhat true of the Renaissance period, but as we now know, the Renaissance was a transitional phase prior to the true modern age.) Or, seeing the rise in disposable wealth, our observer (perhaps having some benevolent leanings of his own) might have said, "The next age will soon abolish the abject poverty of this time, in which many of our citizens are literally in rags in the streets." This prediction would also have been wrong. At the height of the Renaissance many people were still in rags, and several centuries later—far into the modern age—extreme poverty existed in almost every European city. It was not until the late nineteenth century that there was any serious social interest in putting some kind of economic "floor" under the poor. (By this time leading thinkers were already proclaiming the post-modern age.)

This simple example illustrates the folly of linear extrapolation. One cannot deduce the character of the new age by simply projecting selected intellectual, technological, economic, political, and social trends. One can deduce with some reliability *that* a profound social change is underway but not *what* the shape of future society will be.

However, it is useful to have an image of a *possible* future, particularly an image that is consistent with present knowledge and realistically consistent with what one *wants* the future to be. It may be especially helpful to contemplate images of the future that differ from the present in fairly fundamental ways—ways as fundamental as the contemporary "paradigm shift" appears to be. Table 2 on page 96 contrasts one conception of the emerging paradigm with the medieval and modern paradigms. The table is offered as an illustration, not as a prediction, but it is consistent both with what we presently know and with the future of peace that we desire. And it suggests just how fundamental a paradigm change might be.

Reassessing the Possibility of Peace

In spite of the uncertainties involved in projecting an image of the future, there are significant reasons for believing that the hypothesis of transition into the next age may strongly encourage the complete delegitimation of war, *especially if* people want that delegitimation.

In the first place, there is a strong relationship between the five-fold social-movement trend discussed above and the trend toward war's delegitimation. One indication of this is the fact that the peace movement is increasingly linked conceptually with the ecological movement and the value-shift aspect of the women's movement. A high

TABLE 2
A Comparison of Three Paradigms

Sector of Society	Medieval Paradigm (Western Europe)	Current Industrial Paradigm (Industrialized Countries)	One Hypothesized Emerging Paradigm (Global)
Culture, source of meaning (hypothesized)	Traditional and religious institutions prevail; theological rationality; spiritual values are central.	Concepts of material progress, economic production, scientific (measurable) knowledge, manipulative rationality prevail; there is an assumption of separateness from one another and from nature, leading to competiveness and exploitation.	Concepts of human growth and development, learning, community, spirituality prevail. There is a balance of values (masculine/feminine, self-development/ecological; rational intuitive; self-reliance/cooperative; empowerment/nonviolence).
Economy, technology	Secondary importance.	Both are of central importance; technical and economic rationality tend to govern.	The economy is of secondary importance; there is a balance among the three sectors—government, private enterprise, and nonprofit/voluntary.
Social, political	Church as central institution; patriarchal values and assumptions strong.	Primacy of economic/financial/industrial/military institutions; nationalistic; urban.	There is a primacy of community and balance of local/global, urban/rural; emphasis is on local self-reliance, but there is recognition of the need for some global agencies with delimited scope and powers for peacekeeping, care of oceans and atmosphere, etc.

proportion of the people involved with the various social movements mentioned have also been actively involved in the search for peace.

Secondly, there is a strong relationship (if a somewhat less obvious one) between peace and the content of the revolution at the roots of science. Briefly put, that revolution emphasizes the interconnectedness of elements and a "whole-systems" view of reality. As the revolution proceeds, it will become increasingly difficult for thinkers in any field to consider phenomena in isolation. This will also apply to thinking about national security in isolated, us-versus-them terms. A sense of the interconnectedness of the security of all nations and of global security in whole-system terms will follow inevitably from the conceptual revolution in science, whether or not the security thinkers are aware of the derivation.

A third consideration is more subtle still. The time when one age is ending and another opening may well be a time of unusual fluidity in human affairs, a time when people have a greater than ordinary opportunity to shape their future. At most times in history, the main patterns of a culture are relatively stable, and progress (if any) is made within those patterns. The near future is probably *not* such a time. If there is any substance to the hypothesis that the next age in human history is now arriving, then the coming decades can be ones of tremendous change and fluidity. This means that the coming decades may be an unusually favorable time for accomplishing social change, including the delegitimation of war. Again, this argument represents no guarantee of peace because the key factor will be what people decide they want. But it does suggest a subtle and powerful reason why progress toward peace might be able to go further, faster, in the coming decades than most people suppose.

Conclusion

We have spoken in this chapter of the imperative need for the belief in the possibility of peace—the real, emotionally held conviction that "yes, we can do that." We have said that a next major step toward peace is the creation of an image of a future world of peace, an image that is widely credible and ever-more-widely held. We have suggested some elements of that image, important features of a world of the not-distant future that is well on its way toward operational peace.

Many people are skeptical that even this much is realistic. So we have presented, in the latter part of this chapter, two reasons—each important, each often unappreciated—why it *is* realistic.

It is realistic because never before in history has society sought to understand the psychological roots of human behavior in a determined and methodical way. This is the first time that humanity has even begun to uncover systematically the roots of its own behavior and that the general public has taken a serious interest in applying that knowledge to their own lives. In that fact lies a bright promise for the real possibility of peace.

That possibility is also realistic because of the gathering evidence that the present period is the early stage of a transition to a new age. What we may reasonably suppose of the emerging characteristics of that new era strongly supports a belief that sustainable peace is becoming an increasingly plausible future.

If it is true that we are entering a time of historical fluidity, then the images people hold of the future they expect and/or want may have power greater than such images normally have. The way may well be open, therefore, for a kind of "pulling up by humanity's own bootstraps." If people in growing numbers become increasingly convinced of the real possibility of peace, that belief can have great and growing impact. A positive cycle of a tremendously creative and promising kind can be begun. The image of a peaceful future that we are urging in this chapter can help launch that cycle. The good psychological and historical reasons why tremendous progress can be made in the coming decades can and should be incorporated into our image of what those decades *will* be. Because we can be realistically confident that changes truly are possible, we can convincingly imagine or affirm a new future in which they occur. Thereby we convince ourselves and "ourselves" comes to mean an ever-widening group of people.

Furthermore, actual social change comes from people's beliefs and images. There is no place else it can come from. As more and more people truly believe in peace, the belief will make itself true. It will tend to make itself true at one level because these kinds of beliefs will motivate many individuals toward doing the kinds of work that must be done if war is to be delegitimated and peaceful conflict resolution is to take its place. The belief will also make itself true at another, more basic level because social attitudes *are* beliefs and images. If more and more people are convinced, for instance, that in the next age humanity will learn not to use war as a means of resolving conflicts, then that belief itself will make them increasingly reluctant to lend legitimacy to war or preparation for war and indeed war *will* increasingly become irrelevant.

This reasoning is not glib, nor does it involve a "trick of mirrors." The progress toward peace is not a circular, isolated process; it is also part of a larger social change that begins with a recognition that the fundamental social order, of which war is but a small part, is changing.

The delegitimizing of war would be only one aspect of a much more comprehensive shift, which is believed in for its own reasons.

The supporting reasons for the feasibility of peace, coming as they do largely from psychology and history, are good ones. When enough people recognize them, the days that war can still exist will be numbered. Humanity will have found its highest path to peace—the simple recognition that we are already outgrowing war.

Notes

Preface

1. Roger Walsh, *Staying Alive: The Psychology of Human Survival* (Boulder, CO: New Science Library, 1984), p. 1.

Chapter 1

2. A reasonable case can also be made that wars might have ended thereafter, at least in Europe, if the United States had also supported strongly the other half of Wilson's program—the League of Nations.

3. *New York Times*, February 6, 1985, sec. 1.

Chapter 2

4. Willy Brandt, et al., *North-South: A Programme for Survival.* Report of the Independent Commission on International Development Issues (Cambridge, MA: MIT Press, 1980), p. 16.

Chapter 4

5. This paragraph and the four that follow draw upon research done jointly by one of the authors (Smoke) with Dr. William Ury.

Chapter 5

6. Elise Boulding, "Social Imagination and the Crisis of Human Futures: A North American Perspective," *Forum for Correspondence and Contact*, Vol. 13, #2 (February, 1983).

7. Earl Foell and Richard Nenneman, eds. *How Peace Came to the World,* (Cambridge, MA: MIT, 1986).

8. Lewis Mumford, *The Transformations of Man* (New York: Harper & Brothers, 1956), pp. 231 and 248-249.

9. Roger Sperry, "Changing Priorities," *Annual Review of Neuroscience* (Palo Alto, CA: Annual Reviews, Inc., 1981) Vol. 4: pp. 1-15.

For Further Reading

Chapters One Through Four

Barnet, Richard, and Richard Falk, eds. *Security in Disarmament.* Princeton: Princeton University Press, 1965.

Blacker, Coit D., and Gloria Duffy. *International Arms Control: Issues and Agreements.* 2d ed. Stanford: Stanford University Press, 1984.

Boulding, Kenneth E. *Stable Peace.* Austin: University of Texas Press, 1978.

Brandt, Willy, et al. *North-South: A Programme for Survival.* Report of the Independent Commission on International Development Issues (Brandt Commission). Cambridge, MA: MIT Press, 1980.

Brown, Lester R., et al. *State of the World.* New York: W. W. Norton, annual since 1984.

Duedney, Daniel. "Whole Earth Security: A Geopolitics of Peace." *Worldwatch Paper No. 55.* Washington: The Worldwatch Institute. 1983.

Dyson, Freeman. *Weapons and Hope.* New York: Harper & Row, 1984.

Fischer, Dietrich. *Preventing War in the Nuclear Age.* Totowa, NJ: Rowman and Allanheld, 1984.

Freedman, Lawrence. *The Evolution of Nuclear Strategy.* New York: St. Martin's Press, 1981.

Galtung, Johann. *The True Worlds.* New York: The Free Press, 1980.

Heilbroner, Robert. *An Inquiry Into the Human Prospect.* New York: W. W. Norton, 1974.

Johansen, Robert. *Toward an Alternative Security System.* World Policy Paper #24. New York: World Policy Institutes, 1983.

National Academy of Sciences. *Nuclear Arms Control: Background and Issues*. Washington: National Academy Press, 1985.

Osgood, Charles E. *An Alternative to War or Surrender*. Urbana, IL: University of Illinois Press, 1962.

Roberts, Adam. *Nations in Arms: Theory and Practice of Territorial Defense*. London: Chatto and Windus, 1976.

Schell, Jonathan. *The Fate of the Earth*. New York: Alfred A. Knopf, 1982.

Schelling, Thomas C. *Arms and Influence*. New Haven, CT: Yale University Press, 1966.

Sharp, Gene. *Making Europe Unconquerable: The Potential of Civilian-based Deterrence and Defense*. Cambridge, MA: Ballinger, 1985.

Smoke, Richard. *National Security and the Nuclear Dilemma*. 2d ed. New York: Random House, 1987.

Snyder, Glenn H. *Deterrence and Defense*. Princeton: Princeton University Press, 1961.

Sommer, Mark. *Beyond the Bomb: Living Without Nuclear Weapons*. New York: The Talman Company for ExPro Press, 1985.

Stephenson, Carolyn M. *Alternative Methods for International Security*. Washington, D.C.: University Press of America, 1982.

Waltz, Kenneth. *Man, The State, and War*. New York: Columbia University Press, 1959.

Weston, Burns H. *Toward Nuclear Disarmament and Global Security: A Search for Alternatives*. Boulder, CO: Westview Press, 1984.

Chapter 5

Berman, Morris. *The Reenchantment of the World*. Ithaca, NY: Cornell University Press, 1981.

Capra, Fritjof. *The Turning Point*. New York: Bantam, 1983.

Ferguson, Marilyn. *The Aquarian Conspiracy*. Los Angeles: J. P. Tarcher, 1979.

Foell, Earl, and Richard Nenneman, eds. *How Peace Came to the World*. Cambridge, MA: MIT, 1986.

Harman, Willis W., *An Incomplete Guide to the Future*. New York: W. W. Norton, 1976.

Keys, Donald. *Earth at Omega: Passage to Planetization*. Boston: Branden Press, 1982.

Lukacs, John. *The Passing of the Modern Age*. New York: Harper & Row, 1970.

Mumford, Lewis. *Transformations of Man.* New York: Harper & Co., 1956.

Political Psychology (journal). Special issue on the Psychology of the U.S.-Soviet Relationship. June 1985. Vol. 6, no. 2.

Roszak, Theodore. *Person/Planet.* New York: Doubleday, 1978.

Sivard, Ruth Leger. *World Military and Social Expenditures.* Leesburg, VA: WMSE Publications, annual.

Sorokin, Pitirim. *The Crisis of Our Age.* New York: E. P. Dutton, 1951.

Toffler, Alvin. *The Third Wave.* New York: Morrow, 1980; Bantam, 1981.

Wheelis, Allen. *The End of the Modern Age.* New York: Basic Books, 1971.

White, Ralph K. *Psychology and the Prevention of Nuclear War.* New York: New York University Press, 1986.

Whitmont, Edward C. *Return of the Goddess.* New York: Crossroad Publishing Co., 1982.

Index

ABM Treaty. *See* Anti-Ballistic Missile
    Treaty
Afghanistan, 44, 45, 53, 74
Alaska, 18
Algeria, 59
Alternative paths to peace. *See* Paths to
    peace, alternative
American Catholic Bishops, 13-14
Amin, Idi, 50, 68
Annual Review of Neuroscience, 93
Anti-Ballistic Missile Treaty, 13
Aquarian Age. *See* New age
Aquarian Conspiracy, The (Ferguson), 89
Argentina, 21
Arms control, 3, 4(table), 17, 24-30
    disadvantages of, 28-30
    goals of, 24-25, 42
    and nation-states, 56
    as partial nuclear disarmament, 27-28
    and Strategic Defense Initiative, 28
    See also Disarmament; Nuclear
        weapons
Arms race. *See* Arms control; Nuclear
    weapons
Attitudes, changing
    about defense and offense, 63
    and expectations, 66
    about military combat, 64
    and new conflict resolution methods,
        65-67
    about war and peace, 3, 4(table)
    and world opinion, 67. *See also* World
        opinion
    See also New age

Balance of power, 23
Baruch plan, 27
Berman, Morris, 89

Biological Weapons Convention, 25, 27
Boulding, Kenneth, 64
Brandt Commission Report. *See* North-
    South

Canada, 18, 64
    Québecois in, 91
Capra, Fritjof, 89
Causes of war. *See* Human nature;
    International system; Nation-
    states(s); Poverty; Social injustice
Central America, 18
Chemical weapons, 24, 42. *See also*
    Weapons
Chile, 21
Christian Science Monitor, 77
Citizen's army, 43, 44, 45, 46
    as deterrent, 79
    vs. prepared non-violent resistance, 52
    See also Non-violent action
Cold war, 9
Communism
    and class struggle, 31
    Leninist *vs.* Marxist, 19, 66
Concert of Europe, 22-23
    system, 23, 25
Conflict resolution, 55-62, 98. *See also*
    Conflict resolution, alternative
    systems of; Preventive diplomacy
Conflict resolution, alternative systems
    of, 3, 4(table), 55-62, 65, 79
    and changing attitudes, 65-67
    and delegitimation of war, 71
    See also Conflict resolution; Preventive
        diplomacy
Congress of Vienna, 22
Containment, policy of, 19
Crisis of Our Age, The (Sorokin), 89

Crusades, the, 32
Cuban missile crisis, 30
Cyprus, 21
Czechoslovakia, 48

Dancing Wu-Li Masters, The (Zukav), 93
Decline of the West, The (Spengler), 88
Defense, alternative, 3, 4(table), 40-47,
    50
    and deterrence, 42, 46. *See also*
        Deterrence; Deterrence, nuclear
    moderate *vs.* extreme types of, 42-43
    morality of, 43
    and United States, 46
Defensive technology, study team on, 12
Delegitimation of war, 62-65, 71, 79, 98,
    99
    and contemporary social movements,
        93, 95, 97. *See also* Social movements,
        contemporary
    and television, 74
    See also Attitudes, changing; Morality;
        New age; World opinion
Deterrence, 3, 4(table), 11-16, 57, 69
    vs. capacity to defeat enemy, 11-12
    common examples of, 14
    morality of. *See* Morality, of nuclear
        deterrence
    and non-violent actions, 15, 79
    as psychological process, 15
    See also Deterrence, nuclear
Deterrence, nuclear, 11, 20, 42, 69, 80
    vs. common deterrence, 13
    contradiction in, 14, 15
    emotional consequences of, 14
    failure of as policy, 13
    morality of, 13-14
    risks of, 69
    U.S. public support of, 43
    and U.S./USSR relationship, 70
    See also Deterrence; Nuclear weapons
Diplomacy
    goals of, 18
    gunboat, 63
    of intimidation, 18
    See also Preventive diplomacy
Disabled, the, 92
Disarmament, 3, 4(table), 17, 24-30, 70,
    79
    goals of, 24-25
    between World Wars I and II, 26-27
    See also Arms control
Domino theory, 63
Dum-dum bullets, 24

Ecological movement, 91, 93, 95
Einstein, Albert, 1

End of the Modern Age, The (Wheelis),
    89
Ethiopia, 21, 35

Falklands/Malvinas War, 35
Fate of the Earth, The (Schell), 13
Federalism, 32
Ferguson, Marilyn, 89
Finland, 18
Fundamentalism
    Christian, 92
    Moslem, 36
    and social change, 92
Future Security Strategies study team, 12

Gandhi, Mahatma, 15, 47. *See also* Non-
    violent action
Geneva, 18
Geneva Protocol, 24
Genocide, 53
Germany, 8, 20, 26
Goa, 60, 61
Great Britain, 26, 35, 48
Greece, 19
Grenada, 36, 37

Hassan II (king of Morocco), 59
Hegel, Georg Wilhelm Friedrich, 88
Heilbroner, Robert, 34
Hitler, Adolf, 9, 18, 26, 50, 53
Hoffman, Stanley, 86
Homosexuals, 91-92
Human nature
    as cause of war, 31
    See also Psychological research

India, 19, 33, 48, 60. *See also* Gandhi,
    Mahatma
Inquiry Into the Human Prospect, An
    (Heilbroner), 34
International Court of Justice, 21, 56, 59
International law, 8, 13, 20, 21, 60, 65
    and conflict resolution, 56-57
    and Kellogg-Briand Pact, 65
    vs. mediation, 58
International Society of Political
    Psychology, 86
International system
    as cause of wars, 31. *See also* Nation-
        state(s); Poverty; Social injustice
International Telecommunications Union,
    20
Iran-Iraq War, 24, 33, 73
Iraq
    and nuclear weapons, 8
    Osirak nuclear reactor, 7
    See also Iran-Iraq War

Israel, 33
　and Palestinians, 33, 61
　raid on Osirak nuclear reactor, 7-8, 9,
　　10, 15
　and Syria, 19
Italy, 21

Japan, 9, 27, 64
Jews
　and Warsaw Uprising, 86-87
John Paul II. *See* Pope John Paul II

Kashmir, 21, 60
Kellogg-Briand Pact, 27, 65
Khadaffi, Muammar, 35, 50, 68
Khomeini, Ayatollah, 50, 68
King, Martin Luther, Jr., 47, 48
Korea, 64

Law of the Sea Treaty, 18
League of Nations, 21, 26, 27
Lebanon, 53
Limited Test Ban Treaty, 28, 30, 70
Lukacs, John, 89
Lusitania, 8

Maginot Line, 46
Malta, 18
Man, the State, and War (Waltz), 31
Marx, Karl, 88. *See also* Communism
Mediation
　and conflict resolution, 58, 71
Middle Ages, 88, 90, 94, 96(table)
Middle East, 22, 53
Monroe Doctrine, 27
Morality
　and defense, 42, 43
　imperative of, 74
　of non-violence, 49, 51, 68
　of nuclear deterrence, 13-14, 15, 68
　of removing threat to peace, 7, 8, 9-10
Morocco, 59
Mumford, Lewis, 89
Mussolini, Benito, 9, 21

Napoleonic Wars, 23
Nasser, Gamal Abdel, 22
Nation-state(s)
　as cause of wars, 31
　and conflict resolution, 56
　and disarmament/arms-control, 56
　limitations on, 75
　and peaceful invasions, 60-61
NATO. *See* North Atlantic Treaty
　Organization
New age, 98
　predictions of, 88-90

and technology, 87, 90, 92. *See also*
　Technology, rapid evolution
　See also Social movements,
　contemporary
New Zealand, 14
Nicaragua, 18
Nietzsche, Friedrich Wilhelm, 88
Nitze, Paul, 12
Non-Proliferation Treaty, 28, 29, 70
Non-violence. *See* Non-violent action
Non-violent action, 3, 4(table), 47-54, 71
　criticism of, 54
　as deterrent, 15, 79
　examples of, 52-53
　lack of understanding of, 51
　and military invasions, 48, 49, 53
　morality of, 49, 51, 68
　offensive. See Peaceful invasion
　and pacifism, 47
　vs. passive resistance, 47
　and political change, 47-48
　preparation for, 51-52
North and South
　differences in standard of living, 70,
　　79. *See also North-South*; Poverty;
　　Social injustice
North Atlantic Treaty Organization
　(NATO), 41-42, 45
North-South (Brandt Commission
　Report), 34, 35. *See also* North and
　South; Poverty; Social injustice
Nuclear deterrence. *See* Deterrence,
　nuclear
Nuclear testing, 28
Nuclear weapons, 66
　delegitimation, 74
　deployment in Europe, 41
　and freeze movement, 29
　monopoly by United States, 9
　no-first-use, 45
　and nuclear diplomacy, 29
　and nuclear winter, 25
　proliferation, 28, 68, 79. *See also* Non-
　　Proliferation Treaty
　research, 27
　targeting, 41
　See also Deterrence, nuclear
Nuclear winter, 25. *See under* Nuclear
　weapons
Nuremberg trials, 13, 27

OAS. *See* Organization of American
　States
Ogilvy, Jay 94
Okinawa, 44
Operational peace, 2, 67-68, 69, 70, 71
　definition of, 74-75

and image of future, 78-80. *See also*
    Peace, and image of future
See also Peace
Organization of American States (OAS),
    18, 20

Pakistan, 19, 33, 60
Palestinians, 33
Passing of the Modern Age, The (Lukacs),
    89
Paths to peace, alternative, 3, 4(table)
    characteristics of, 39
    See also Operational peace; Peace
Peace
    as absence of nuclear threat, 3
    belief in possibility of, 75-78, 79, 80-81,
        90, 95
    complete, 2, 75
    conferences, 26
    degrees of, 2, 73-75
    identified with arms control, 29
    and image of future, 76-80, 98. *See also*
        New age
    imaging of, 85-86
    maintaining, 55
    movement, 95, 97. *See also* Social
        movements, contemporary
    nine paths to, 3-4
    and nuclear deterrence, 14. *See also*
        Deterrence, nuclear
    operational. *See* Operational peace
    positive and negative definitions of, 2
    removing threats to, 7-10
    stable, 64
    See also Delegitimation of war
Peaceful invasion, 59-61
Peacekeeping forces, unofficial, 61
Pearl Harbor, 10
Person/Planet (Roszak), 89
Polisario Front, 59
Pope John Paul II, 13-14
Portugal, 60
Poverty
    as cause of war, 34-35. *See also* North
        and South; Social injustice
Preventive diplomacy, 3, 4(table), 17,
    18-24
    and world opinion, 70, 80
    See also Conflict resolution,
        alternative systems of
Psychological research
    and depth psychology, 83-84
    limitations of, 86
    and perception and attribution, 82-83
    and primacy of inner conscious
        awareness, 93

and reprogramming unconscious mind,
    85
and unconscious programming, 84-85

Rambo, 64
Reagan, Ronald, 12
Red Baron, 64
Reenchantment of the World, The
    (Berman), 89
Renaissance, the, 94, 95
Roman Empire, 9, 11, 90
Roszak, Theodore, 89
Russell, Bertrand, 9

Sabotage, acts of, 52, 53
SALT. *See* Strategic Arms Limitation
    Talks
Schell, Jonathan, 13, 74
Schopenhauer, Arthur, 88, 93
Schwartz, Peter, 94
SDI. *See* Strategic Defense Initiative
Social and Cultural Dynamics (Sorokin),
    89
Social injustice, 79
    as cause of wars, 32-37
    See also North and South; Poverty
Social movements, contemporary
    and delegitimation of war, 93. *See also*
        Delegitimation of war
    and paradigm changes, 94, 95,
        96(table)
    trends in, 91-93
    See also Attitudes, change; New age
Sorokin, Pitirim, 89
South Africa, 21
Soviet Union
    and Baruch plan, 27
    and biological weapons, 25
    and Goa, 60
    invasion of Czechoslovakia, 48
    Nazi invasion of, 86
    and Non-Proliferation Treaty, 29
    and nuclear deterrence, 11, 70
    and preventive diplomacy, 20, 22
    preventive war against, 9, 10
    and U.S. naval units, 22
    and West Germany, 18
Spain, 59
Spanish American War, 9
Spanish Sahara, 59, 61
Spengler, Oswald, 88
Sperry, Roger, 93
Star Wars. *See* Strategic Defense
    Initiative
Strategic Arms Limitation Talks (SALT),
    28, 29, 70

Strategic Defense Initiative (SDI), 12, 13
  and arms control talks, 28
  for Europe, 46
Supersonic transport (SST), 92
Sweden, 18, 19
Switzerland, 18, 19
Syria, 19

Tao of Physics, The (Capra), 93
Technology
  and deterrence, 12
  and new age, 87, 90, 92
  offensive *vs.* defensive, 45
  rapid evolution, 30, 42
Television, 74
Terrorism, 9, 10, 13, 68
Third Wave, The (Toffler), 89
Third World, 22, 23, 36
  and gunboat diplomacy, 63
  poverty in, 34, 35
  See also North and South
Thirty Years War, 32
Toffler, Alvin, 89
Toynbee, Arnold, 88
Transformation of Man, The (Mumford), 89
Turkey, 19
Turning Point, The (Capra), 89

UN. *See* United Nations
UNESCO. *See* United Nations Education, Scientific and Cultural Organization
United Nations, 2, 18, 20, 32
  General Assembly, 21
  Security Council, 21, 27, 56-57, 60
United Nations Educational, Scientific and Cultural Organization (UNESCO), 82
United States, 8, 9, 10, 15, 18, 24, 25, 26
  and alternative defense, 46. *See also* Defense, alternative
  and Asia, 63
  and Baruch plan, 27
  Blacks and Hispanics in, 91
  and Canada, 64
  civil rights movement in, 48
  invasion of Grenada, 36, 37
  monopoly of nuclear weapons, 9, 27
  and Non-Proliferation Treaty, 29
  and nuclear deterrence, 11, 19, 70. *See also* Deterrence, nuclear
  policy of containment, 19-20
  and preventive diplomacy, 23
  and Russian naval units, 22
  and Third World, 35
  and Vietnam War, 10, 36, 37, 63, 92. *See also* Vietnam War

University for Peace, 2
USSR. *See* Soviet Union

Vatican, 21
Viet Cong, 44. *See also* Vietnam War
Vietnam-Kampuchea War, 33
Vietnam War, 10, 36, 37, 42, 44, 63, 64, 73, 92
Waltz, Kenneth, 31
War(s), 23, 31, 81, 82
  causal theories of, 31-32
  conventional, 41-42
  delegitimation of. *See* Delegitimation of war
  eliminating causes of, 3, 4(table), 17, 31-37
  Falkland/Malvinas, 35
  future, 34, 42
  Iran-Iraq, 24, 33, 73
  policy wars, 36-37
  and poverty. *See* Poverty
  preventive, 9, 10, 24
  and social injustice. *See* Social injustice
  Thirty Years, 32
  Vietnam-Kampuchea, 33
  See also Vietnam War, World War I; World War II
Warsaw Pact, 41, 42, 45
Warsaw Uprising, 86-87
Washington Conference (1921), 30
Weapons
  conventional, 41, 42, 66, 70
  limited to defensive use, 79
  See also Chemical weapons; Nuclear weapons
Wheelis, Allen, 89
Whole systems view of reality, 94, 97
Wilson, Woodrow, 8, 9
Women's movement, 92, 95
World confederation, 32
World Disarmament Conference (1932), 26
World Health Organization, 20, 34
World opinion, 56, 67
  and peaceful invasion of Goa, 60. *See also* Goa
  and preventive diplomacy, 70, 80. *See also* Preventive diplomacy
World War I, 23, 24, 64
  and public revulsion, 27-28, 30
World War II, 20, 24, 44, 64, 86

Zukav, Gary, 93

The Institute of Noetic Sciences

The Institute of Noetic Sciences was founded in 1973 by Edgar D. Mitchell, Apollo 14 astronaut, to engage in research, dialogue and communication on issues concerning the human mind and consciousness and their role in the continuing evolution of humankind.

Major programs include:

Global Mind Change

Many indicators point to a fundamental change of mind occurring around the world, driven by a complex of interconnected global problems and pulled by an emerging vision of a positive global future. Although the full nature of this transformation is not yet apparent, it clearly involves reassessment of the scientific understanding of the human mind and spirit; of our ecological relationship to the planet; of the assurance of peace and common security; and of the role of business in creating a meaningful and viable future.

The Institute is involved in cooperation with numerous other organizations in various aspects of helping this change be a smooth and nondisruptive transformation. One of the most critical areas is the achievement of global peace. Activities here include participation in an international project on alternate security; promoting a positive view of the achievability of peace; tours to the Soviet Union and other countries with opportunities for cross-cultural dialogues and "citizen diplomacy"; and a booklet by Willis Harman entitled "How to Think About Peace", which is part of a *Peace Packet*. The *Peace Packet* is available from the Institute.

Inner Mechanisms of the Healing Response

Creating a scientific understanding of the mind/body relationship has been a fundamental goal of the Institute. Early work focused on verifying the importance of the link between mind and body through support of practitioners of alternative techniques. Currently, the Institute is operating a research program devoted to studying the mechanisms of the healing response. What are the innate processes within us that stimulate recovery and natural self-repair? Is there an unknown healing system that promotes remission from normally fatal illnesses? The Inner Mechanisms Program supports proposals from selected researchers and supports targeted interdisciplinary working conferences on mechanisms of healing.

Program areas include:
• *Psychoneuroimmunology.* What are the systems of linkage between the mind, the brain, and the immune system? Can these links mediate self-healing in a significant way?
• *Spontaneous remission.* What is the evidence for the existence of spontaneous remission? Which kinds of diseases are more "remission prone"? Which kinds of people experience remission and why? The Institute has created the largest medical database on remission and will soon begin to track the incidence of remission in the United States.
• *Spiritual healing.* Do prayer, meditation and spiritual beliefs affect healing, and if so, how? What is the psychophysiology of reported instances of "miraculous" healing?
• *Bio-energetic or energy medicine.* Are there measurable magnetic and electrical fields around or inside the body that can aid in our understanding of healing mechanisms? Will further understanding of the body's electrical fields and circuits provide major new understanding of the healing system?

Exceptional Abilities

What are the inner and outer limits of human ability? Is each of us capable of extraordinary achievement, and if so, what are the keys to it? How can exceptional abilities be trained, and what are the implications of new knowledge about them? Answers to these questions—advances in our understanding of "the farther reaches of human nature"—could help define a new, vital vision of human possibilities and renew commitment to positive individual and social goals.

Exceptional abilities include *ordinary capacities developed to an outstanding degree,* such as lightning calculation or photographic memory, and *anomalous and paranormal capacities.* They also include *exceptional achievement* as manifested in creative genius or in the cultivation of heroic character traits such as creative altruism, and *extraordinary systemic transformations* such as spontaneous remission and unusual voluntary control of mind/body functions. These abilities challenge both the adequacy of existing scientific models of human functioning and individual beliefs about the limits of personal excellence and achievement. Research and education to discover more about the nature, mechanisms and scope of exceptional abilities could have far-reaching implications for scientific policy and research; learning and performance in business, education and sports; individual health and well-being; and social values and beliefs.

The Institute is presently working to:

- *Establish a database.* Who demonstrates exceptional abilities? How have their abilities been documented or studied—and what were the findings?
- *Develop a research agenda.* Which abilities, if understood better, would have the greatest significance for science and society? What are the most promising ways to study them?
- *Sponsor public symposia and scientific roundtables.* By fostering dialogue, can we inspire new public and professional interest in extraordinary and still largely untapped potentials of the human mind, body, and spirit?
- *Support cutting-edge research.* Which studies might pioneer advances in theory and practice about constructive human capacities and characteristics—and how can the Institute support them?
- *Publish information about new findings.* Through timely reporting of advances in the theory and investigation of exceptional abilities, as well as new developments in their application, we hope to broaden interest in the field of extended human capabilities and promote optimal human learning and development.

The Institute's pioneering research, communication and networking activities are financed almost completely by donations from members and other sources of private support. A nonprofit organization, the Institute is open to general membership.

Members are kept abreast of the latest progress in these major new fields of study. Members receive regular publications featuring exciting insights into the work of leading investigators, in-depth articles on critical aspects of consciousness research, announcements of forthcoming conferences, presentations, and tours, reviews of new publications, and the opportunity to order books and tapes at a discount directly from the Institute.

Members from the world over join in supporting research that is moving toward understanding and enhancing the quality of life for us all.

For information on becoming a member of the Institute, please send your request to:

The Institute of Noetic Sciences
475 Gate Five Road, Suite 300
Sausalito, CA 94966-0097
(415) 331-5650

DATE DUE

OCT 3 1988			
JUN 0 5 1989			
MAR 2 5 1991			
GAYLORD			PRINTED IN U.S.A